CV

One Perfect Day

Also by Diane Burke

Hidden in Plain View
Double Identity
Silent Witness
Midnight Caller
Bounty Hunter Guardian
Danger in Amish Country (with Marta Perry
and Kit Wilkinson)

One Perfect Day

A Mother and Son's Story of Adoption
and Reunion

DIANE BURKE
with
STEVE ORLANDI

SKYHORSE PUBLISHING

MEMOIRS BY DEFINITION are a written depiction of events in somebody's life. They are memories. All of the events in this story are as accurate and truthful as possible. Many names and places have been changed to protect the privacy of others. Mistakes, if any, are caused solely by the passage of time.

Skyhorse Publishing books may be purchased in bulk at special discounts for sales promotion, corporate gifts, fund-raising, or educational purposes. Special editions can also be created to specifications. For details, contact the Special Sales Department, Skyhorse Publishing, 307 West 36th Street, 11th Floor, New York, NY 10018 or info@skyhorsepublishing.com.

Skyhorse® and Skyhorse Publishing® are registered trademarks of Skyhorse Publishing, Inc.®, a Delaware corporation.

www.skyhorsepublishing.com

10 9 8 7 6 5 4 3 2 1

Library of Congress Cataloging-in-Publication Data is available on file.
Burke, Diane, 1951-
   One perfect day : a mother and son's story of adoption and reunion / Diane Burke with Steve Orlandi.
      pages cm
   ISBN 978-1-62873-779-0 (hardback)
1. Burke, Diane. 2. Orlandi, Steve. 3. Birthparents--United States--Identification. 4. Birthmothers--United States--Biography. 5. Adoptees--United States--Biography. 6. Adoptees--United States--Identification. I. Orlandi, Steve. II. Title.
   HV874.82.B87A3 2014
   362.82'98--dc23
                              2013044412

Printed in the United States of America

Dear Reader,

Adoption reunions are high-octane events. Emotions and expectations are hard to put into words. When my mother and I talked about the possibility of writing this book, our intention was twofold:

In a world filled with bad news, we wanted to share something uplifting, something inspirational. We also wanted to share our experiences with others contemplating reunions because it isn't an easy path but, at least in our case, it was one well worth the journey.

Imagine my surprise when I discovered my mother was an accomplished author and had the professional skills to reenact our lives with such accuracy and truth. Now I know where I get my creative side.

I am proud of my mother and I was very happy to help her fill in the missing pieces of this story.

I hope you enjoy reading the story as much as we are enjoying living it.

Steve

p.s. My mom wants me to let you know her author page can be found at www.amazon.com/author/dianeburke and her email address is diane@dianeburkeauthor.com. She loves hearing from her readers so go ahead and write her. Mothers! LOL

Acknowledgments

FIRST AND FOREMOST, I want to thank Nicole Resciniti, my agent, and Nicole Frail, my editor, who believed in this project and stood up against the marketers who told them that since I was an ordinary person and not a celebrity, this book would never sell. I hope my readers reward them for their belief in us.

I wish to thank Barbara Orlandi and Kristin McKnight for encouraging and supporting Steve every step of this journey. I love you both.

I wish to thank Nancy and Joe Orlandi for doing an awesome job of raising "our" son and for opening your hearts and your family to include me. I will be forever grateful.

I wish to thank my sons, David and Dan, for taking this journey with me and welcoming Steve into our family.

I wish to thank my brothers, Michael and Brendan, who didn't worry about embarrassment, who stood by my side during periods of family derision and defended my right to tell this story.

I want to thank Dan "Flannagan" for encouraging me to write this truthfully even though it didn't show him in the best light. He's become the man I always knew he could be. He loves the Lord, loves his sons, is a good grandfather, and we have become good friends.

And last, but certainly not least, I want to thank my son, Steve Orlandi, who began a search not knowing where the road would lead, held on through the storms, and loved a mother who wasn't the white-picket-fence mom he had hoped to find but loved her anyway. I love you, son. You've changed my life in more ways than you will ever really know.

In God's time, in God's way, is God's plan.

Prologue

SOMETIMES IT IS the simplest of things—making a right turn instead of a left, accepting an unexpected invitation, stopping to help someone on the side of the road—that can change the entire course of your life.

I stood at the mailbox kiosk in my Florida development on a beautiful, warm April afternoon and had one of those inconsequential moments that should've meant nothing and yet . . . would soon mean everything.

Leafing through the mail, there was a slip of paper stating a certified letter waited for me at the post office. Thinking it was some kind of elaborate marketing ploy like the one that sends you a car key in the mail and tells you to just show up at the dealership and see if this key fits a lock, I tossed the slip in the console drawer as I climbed back into my car and didn't give it another thought.

A few days later, on my way to the grocery store, that ragged, crumpled slip of paper poked out from the drawer and I decided to pick up the package. I had to show my photo identification and sign for it before the clerk handed me a nondescript white envelope. I remember thinking that if this was a scam or a request from some organization looking for a hefty charitable donation, they were going to a lot of trouble and expense to do it.

As soon as I stepped out of the post office, I opened the envelope and withdrew the letter, which read:

Dear Mrs. Burke,

We have been trying unsuccessfully to reach you on a very personal matter. This will be our last attempt to contact you. Please call us at (phone number) between the hours of 9:00 and 5:00, Monday through Friday.

I stared at the letter in my hands. Now I was more than curious. No one had tried to contact me. What were they talking about? Who was this person and what did they want?

When I got home, I immediately went into my home office and dialed the number. I asked for the person who had signed the letter. I still had no idea what this was about. My imagination was flying—but not even my wildest imagination could have prepared me for the shock of what was to come.

Every sixty seconds that I was kept on hold, the switchboard operator would come back on the line. She'd apologize that the person I was trying to reach was still on the phone and ask me to leave my phone number. Still believing that I was involved in some elaborate hoax, I refused to leave my number and told her I would continue to wait.

When she came back on the line for the fifth time, my patience was wearing thin.

"Are you sure you won't leave me your telephone number?" she asked. "I'm sure Ms. Fowler will call you as soon as she finishes her call."

"No, thanks. It seems to me this woman went to a lot of trouble to find me. I'll wait a little longer, but when I do hang up, I won't be calling back."

"No! Wait! Please don't hang up. She'll be right with you."

I was put on hold again.

Seconds later, a woman's voice came on the line. "This is Patricia Fowler. I'm so sorry to keep you waiting. I was tied up on another line. Is this Diane Burke?"

"Yes. What is this about?"

"Mrs. Burke, I promise to answer all of your questions, but will you bear with me for just a few minutes more and answer some of mine?"

I was hesitant but said okay.

"Was your maiden name Diane Bradford?"

"Yes."

"Did you attend Kinnelon High School?"

"Yes." I smiled. I was right. They wanted money; it had to be an alumni collection.

"Do you have six brothers and sisters?"

A chill ran down my spine. This wasn't any ordinary telephone call or a request for a charitable donation.

"Who is this and what do you want?" I demanded, annoyance quickly turning into anger and maybe just a little bit of fear.

In a very soft, gentle voice, Pat Fowler asked, "Mrs. Burke, did you give up a child for adoption in 1971?"

I collapsed into my desk chair. It took me a moment to respond.

"Yes," I whispered, my voice laced with tears.

Chapter

1

THERE IS NO such thing as a perfect family. Mainly because families are made of people and everyone knows people aren't perfect. All families, even the best ones, have their idiosyncrasies, their varying degrees of dysfunction, and they have all mastered the ability to keep secrets.

Sometimes the secrets are innocent, can stay secrets forever and don't hurt anyone. Like the fact that their first child's birthday comes eight weeks shy of nine months into the marriage. Or that big, strong dad is afraid of spiders and bugs. Or that money is tighter than the neighbors might think and mom's parents have padded the home funds multiple times.

Sometimes the secrets are hurtful, can fester beneath the surface for decades and end up damaging lives. Like the secrets that hide emotional, physical, or sexual abuse. Or the ones that hide dishonesty, infidelity, and betrayal.

All families harbor secrets, and mine was no exception.

I grew up in a typical middle class family in the days when mothers stayed home, ran the house, and raised the children while fathers labored forty-plus hours a week earning the money to support the household.

My father's job in retail management required us to move frequently. The company didn't give raises. It gave promotions, which always meant a different store in a different location to earn that salary bump and move up the ladder. I think the longest we ever stayed in one place was two years. So I never felt I had a home or roots. When people asked me where I was from, I used to chuckle and say, "All over."

Some of my siblings had no difficulty with the moves. They made friends wherever we went and adjusted well to the many different schools. One brother excelled in it so well he spent his adult life working and traveling throughout Europe and exposed his daughters to a multitude of cultures, languages, and religions that served them well when they became adults.

I wish I could say the same for myself.

The moves were hard on me. Constantly having to leave friends and comfort zones behind and forge new ones didn't make me outgoing or leadership material. I truly wish it had. I know hundreds of thousands of military families face those challenges all the time and I respect and admire their resiliency.

For me, the frequent moves made me uncomfortable in new situations. The loss of the friends I'd made in the prior city made me less willing to try and make new friends in the new ones. As far back as I can remember, I haven't handled loss well. If I had learned how to say good-bye and move on when I was a child, I might be able to look back and say those moves helped prepare me for what was to come.

But good-byes were never easy for me under any circumstances.

I had no idea during those childhood years that the hardest good-bye I would ever have to face was still to come.

It wasn't until I had married and left home that my father switched jobs and the Bradfords were able to put down roots.

My middle and younger siblings got to attend the same school from beginning to end, graduate, and make friends who lasted from grade school through college. They actually had the opportunity to think of one location as home.

My parents lived in their Oakland, Michigan, house for more than twenty years. For all of us, even the older ones who moved out on their own years before, when we traveled home for holidays and special occasions, this particular house became our gathering place.

The big white house on the hill that called to each one of us, that housed us during Thanksgivings and Christmases, that heard the echo of grandchildren's feet racing through the halls and down the stairs, became our Bradford roots.

We used to joke that that house was Mom's Tara from *Gone with the Wind*. She'd been raised in a row home in Philadelphia. Her life's ambition was to do more, be more, and have more. She cared deeply about her social standing and what the neighbors thought.

This house was her pride and joy. Her stamp of success.

I'm happy that she attained it.

Everyone has dreams in life. Not everyone sees them come true.

Society was different when my parents were first married. No one asked women if they were happy staying home with the children. No one encouraged women to have careers. In poor families, like my mother's had been, the choice to go to college was offered to the first-born son and was never even a remote possibility for a daughter.

At the age of sixteen, my mother met my father and fell in love. At nineteen, they married. I was born exactly nine months later.

My mother never liked or wanted children, but she had seven of them.

She would have made a fabulous CEO of a large company if she'd been given the chance. She was an intelligent woman with business savvy who read voraciously and kept herself up-to-date on politics and current affairs. She was well-liked in social settings and I truly believe she would have blossomed and thrived if she had been afforded the opportunity to have a career when she was young.

Instead I'd often hear her say she had to watch "weak men," probably referring to her brother who was given the opportunity to go to college, make stupid business decisions while she was stuck at home with a brood of kids reminding her that this wasn't the life she'd dreamed about but one she couldn't escape.

My mother adjusted to her life at home. Of seven children, she even found two of them she liked enough to earn the title "mom's favorites" from the rest of us. Mom fed us, clothed us, raised us, and criticized us without mercy. She was the queen of taking whatever glimmer of accomplishment or pride you had in yourself and beating it into the ground so you felt inferior and worthless.

For some reason I never understood, and to this day my siblings haven't figured it out either, I was also one of Mom's favorites—her favorite one to hate.

That's probably a harsh statement. I don't like to think my mother actually hated me. I'd like to think the softer side of my mother, which I saw outside the doors of our home in social circles or with strangers on the street, would have prevented her from ever feeling hatred for anyone.

But she sure did carry a very, very heavy dislike for me.

Even though we were oil and water, we were also mother and daughter. Although I didn't always like my mother, I loved her. She wasn't perfect. Neither am I. She made some terrible mistakes in her life. So have I. I helped care for her in the final days of her life. I sat by her bedside with my father and siblings until she died. I visit her grave occasionally. And I miss her.

She was my mother.

A part of me and me a part of her.

Sometimes I catch a glimpse of her when I look at my reflection in the mirror. Or I've heard the echo of her voice when I scolded my children with idle threats like "Get in that bed or I'm coming up there."

So I am *not* trying to bash my mother.

She did the best she could being the person she was and dealing with the circumstances facing her.

I understand that.

But if this is to be a truthful depiction of events, a true testament of how one person's decisions can so negatively impact another person's life, then I have to discuss my mother—and myself—and the choices we made.

I was eighteen and had just finished my first year of college when I met Steve's father. I had gotten a summer job on the assembly line of a plastics plant packing trash bags. Steve's father was a year older and it was his job to keep the machines up and running. On a visa from a foreign country, I found him fascinating and, for me, it was definitely love at first sight.

I was nineteen and four months pregnant before I had the courage to tell my mother. But . . . the truth is that I never had to tell her. One afternoon I was sitting on the side of my bed. She was standing in the hallway. She looked at me, really looked at me, and she knew. I will never forget the expressions racing across her face, the shock, the disbelief, the shame, and finally the rage.

"Are you pregnant?" she screamed at me from my bedroom's open doorway.

Terrified, I couldn't find my voice to answer.

"Are you?" She stared at me with such anger—and what, to this day, I truly believe was hatred. Her voice dropped to a whisper. "How could you do this to your father and me?" Without another word, she turned and walked away.

That evening, my siblings in bed for the night or otherwise scattered, my mother sat in her usual chair in the living room reading one of her many mystery books, or at least feigning to read. I don't think either of us could concentrate on anything that night. I sat at the dining room table. She hadn't spoken a word to me since the morning's accusation. Neither of us looked at each other or spoke. We just waited for Dad to come home from work.

My mother had called him earlier and prepared him for the situation he was walking into. I heard the garage door go up and my pulse began to race. We lived in a split-level house and I could hear his slow, heavy footsteps as he made his way up the two short flights of stairs. My heart beat so hard I thought it would push through my chest. Tears burned my eyes no matter how hard I tried not to cry.

The doctor I had seen when I suspected I was pregnant had referred me to one of the few New York clinics that performed abortions in those days. This was before *Roe v. Wade*, but there were still doctors who handled abortion quietly. The obstetrician who ended up delivering my son was also known by word-of-mouth for performing abortions in the first trimester of pregnancy. I remember wearing a poncho on my first visit to him, and when I sat in his office for the initial interview, he asked what I wanted. When he realized how far along I was in my pregnancy, he became my obstetrician, not my abortionist.

I had had an appointment with the New York doctor when I'd first learned of my pregnancy. It would have been so easy. No one would have ever known and this little "mistake" would be over.

But this wasn't a "mistake."

Not to me.

It was a tiny little baby. Even at this early stage of pregnancy, I already possessed a love and a feeling of protectiveness for this child that was stronger than anything I had ever known.

Even though my father's footsteps drew nearer, while my mother sat glaring at me and I knew my life was definitely about to change, I wasn't then, and have never been, sorry that I chose life for this child. It's probably the one, right, good decision I ever made.

The ensuing conversation with my parents was difficult and painful. They were angry, understandably so, and hurt and stressed to the hilt. I will never forget my father's final reaction. He stood with his back to me at the kitchen sink and poured himself a glass of water.

"We'll put the child up for adoption," my mother said. "I spoke to my brother today and he's willing to help us set things up."

My father threw his glass in the sink. He spun around and looked at both of us, his eyes glistening with unshed tears. "Sure!" he yelled. "Let's just give it away! It's just a puppy that nobody wants, right?"

He stormed out of the kitchen and down the hall toward his room.

I don't know what broke my heart more: seeing how much I had hurt my father or realizing for the first time what my mother intended to do with my child.

◦◦◦

All families have secrets—and this was a big one. My siblings were told I had moved to Atlantic City to live by the beach with my uncle and his family. My grandparents were told I had found a lucrative secretarial job in Atlantic City. That was the story my mother spun to the neighbors, too.

Like all lies, there was a grain of truth in my mother's words.

I did stay in Atlantic City with my uncle for a couple of weeks while arrangements were made for me to be placed in a home for unwed mothers. It was a nice old house on a shaded, quiet street. It had a stone front, a large enclosed front porch, a flower-bordered sidewalk to a side entrance. I think what surprised me the most about it when my uncle dropped me off out front was that there wasn't a sign.

I don't know what I had been expecting. Maybe a billboard that screamed UNWED MOTHERS INSIDE, COME TAKE A PEEK. There was nothing so dramatic or definitive about the house. There was simply a wooden post with a black iron house number hanging from it.

For the first time through this whole experience, I felt nervous as I stood outside and rang the bell. The reality of the situation hit me hard. I would be living in a city far away from my home, friends, and family. I would be living with strangers. I would be housed with mothers who also would be losing their babies. I would be totally alone. And I was scared.

The two women, or house mothers who ran the home, were the sweetest women God ever made. Compassionate. Non-judgmental. Kind. Both women were in their seventies, retired and supplementing their retirement income by living in the home with the girls, doing the grocery shopping, doing the cooking, and making sure all the girls got to their doctor's appointments and eventually to the hospital when the time came to deliver.

The upstairs had been turned into two huge rooms with six twin beds in each. We all shared one shower, one bath. There was another bathroom downstairs. Each of the matrons had a private bedroom and bath downstairs as well.

One of the elderly women, the one with snow white hair, metal glasses, and an ever-present smile, reminded me of pictures of Mrs. Santa Claus I'd seen as a child. She showed me to my room. Mrs. K would turn out to be the only friend I made the entire four and a half months I was a resident of the home. She took me under her wing. She'd play 500 Rummy with me in the evenings after chores. Trying not to upset any of the other girls by showing favoritism, she'd sneak me out of the house, occasionally, and take me to Bingo with her. I truly loved that woman.

You'd think that the twelve girls in the house would have become good friends. We were all in the same boat. We were all going through the hardships and discomforts of pregnancy. We were all away from family and friends. We were all still smarting from the breakups we'd had with our boyfriends. We were all facing the inevitability of having to give our children away.

You'd think with so much in common we'd develop a strong bond. We didn't.

The misery we felt inside we manifested on each other.

Newbies were cruelly initiated into the house.

I remember more than one night when I had to lay atop towels because one of the girls had soaked my mattress. Or I had my clothes and towels mysteriously disappear when I was taking a shower and would have to walk back to my room dripping and naked. Or I'd have my plate "accidentally" knocked out of my hand when someone passed me on the way to the dining room.

I came to realize these incidents weren't aimed specifically at me. They tormented me only until one of the girls delivered. Once a position was open and the next girl came into the house, then I was left alone and they moved on to the new girl.

Not all the girls participated in this type of hazing. Most of us minded our own business and kept to ourselves. I know I was just as guilty as the other girls when I didn't try to stop the tormentors or try to make friends with the girls who arrived after me.

I have no excuse other than to say I was in pain . . . deep, dark emotional pain . . . and the only way I could cope with feeling deserted by my boyfriend, deserted by my family, and scared to death of the future was to hide inside myself.

The only person in this world who I loved was my baby and I knew without doubt that this baby would love me back. It would be the two of us against the world and it would be all right.

Many nights, I'd lie awake staring into the darkness, afraid, confused, unsure, but never alone. I had my baby. I'd rub a comforting circle on my stomach as my baby moved and kicked within me. I'd hum a lullaby, never sure whether I was comforting the baby or myself until we'd both fall asleep.

It didn't take long for me to adjust to the schedules and routines in the house. We'd all have chores listed on a chart on the wall. Some of us helped in the kitchen to prepare meals. Others cleaned up afterward. Some ran the vacuum throughout the downstairs. Others were on bathroom clean-up detail. Once a week the chores would be rotated so no one could complain about the jobs they were assigned, although everyone complained anyway.

Every two weeks, some of us went grocery shopping with one of the house matrons. Looking back, I'm sure we were quite a sight: an elderly matron leading the way, pushing a grocery cart, with at least three pregnant girls following single file behind her. The store manager would greet us. He'd open a cash register just for us (and our four overflowing grocery carts) and then he'd have a couple of his stock clerks help us load our van.

There was a psychologist, Mr. D., who maintained an office in the basement. His office hours were posted on the door leading downstairs. He'd come up periodically, ask the group as a whole (usually from the dining room doorway as we were gathered for breakfast) how we were doing, and reminded us that his door was always open if any of us wanted to talk.

In the 1960s and early '70s, society operated under the mindset that the only sensible thing to do with an unwed mother was to place her child up for adoption. Children deserved a two-parent loving home and a teenage single mother couldn't possibly meet the child's needs, so there wasn't any further discussion. No one suggested or encouraged other alternatives. In my world, unwed mothers were worse than the fictional heroine wearing a scarlet A. I was never sure whether it was falling in love and engaging in sex before marriage that was the sin deserving punishment—or if it was getting caught.

I truly believe social workers and psychologists in those days were trained to encourage unwed mothers to give the children away and little thought was given to the emotional or psychological needs of the mother. I believe that at that time in history society truly believed it was acting in the best interests of both mother and child when it encouraged adoption and offered limited or no alternatives. By keeping this secret, by aiding and abetting the placement of the child, society was, in fact, giving the child a good home and the mother a second chance, a chance to go on with life and get it right this time.

So everyone covered it up, lied about it, hid it, and encouraged the mother to just get on with her life and pretend it never happened. *Pretend.* It's a simple word but it can cause a world of emotional damage and pain.

I'll never understand this line of thinking.

If a married woman carried a child to term and experienced a stillborn delivery, society would have rallied around that mother. There would have been a wake and a funeral for a sense of closure. There would have been family and friends gathering to show their support and offer comfort. There would have been telephone calls and visits in the months afterward to help that mother move past her grief.

Why didn't anyone think that an unwed mother would experience loss?

Didn't that unwed mother just carry a child for nine months, endure the pain of labor and delivery and then have that child taken away? Why didn't anyone realize that for this mother, placing this child up for adoption, either willingly or unwillingly, would still result in a similar devastating loss?

Only for unwed mothers there'd be no help.

There would be no support groups where the pain could be discussed and healing begun. There would be no sense of closure because everyone, including the mother, would know that child still existed somewhere out there in the world. There would be no comfort offered from family or friends because the unwed mother had brought shame to them.

So it was no surprise to me that Mr. D. didn't have anyone beating down his door to talk.

But I did talk to him once—about how to build a kite.

He actually spent an hour with me trying to put together an elaborate kite that I could fly on the beach.

A kite!

I look back now and want to shake him silly. Why didn't he encourage me to talk? Why didn't he ask even one question about how I felt or how I was doing? Why didn't he once ask how I was adjusting to the idea that I would be placing my child up for adoption?

Any of those questions would have opened a flood gate that I wouldn't have been able to close. All those questions lived inside my head and my heart twenty-four hours a day. I was afraid. I felt alone and unloved. I felt there wasn't an adult in the world I could trust or talk to.

With the slightest encouragement, I would have talked. Most likely I would have burst into tears and talked and talked and talked until there wasn't another word or breath left inside of me. He was the adult. He was the professional. Yet, the only time I ever spent with him was the day we built a kite.

He was a great kite builder.

Chapter

2

THE GIRLS IN the home were mothers-to-be. They were also young, teenage girls ranging in age from twelve to nineteen—silly, immature, and still interested in boys despite their bulging bodies. Some of the girls would sneak off and meet their boyfriends on the beach. Nobody ever told the house matrons, probably because we were envious and wishing it could be us.

One girl in particular took her boy-crazy days to the extreme. She'd head to the beach before the lifeguards arrived. She'd dig a huge hole in front of the lifeguard station, lay on the ground with her belly in the hole, and then flirt for hours with whatever young lifeguard showed up for duty.

Seeing some of the girls sneaking around with their boyfriends or flirting with the lifeguards made me miss my boyfriend terribly.

One afternoon I decided to call him at work.

When he came on the line, he immediately asked me where I was. I couldn't tell him. My mother had threatened both of us that if he ever contacted me again she would have him deported since he was here on a visa from a foreign country. I realize now that had been an idle threat. There was nothing she could have done to either one of us. I wasn't legally a minor and he was a year older than me. However, we honestly didn't realize at the time that she couldn't make good on those threats.

When he came to the phone, just the sound of his voice filled me with hope . . . hope that I'd hear him say everything was going to be okay and that somehow we'd work it out and be together as a family. I'd dated other boys in high school but he was different. He was my one, all-consuming, passionate teenage love.

When I met him, he was working and attending college on a visa here in the United States. I had a job on an assembly line earning money for college. He worked in the same plant for the same reason and fixed the machines when they'd break down, which they did at least once during each shift.

I thought he was so handsome. He stood about 5'10" and although not tall, he was solid and strong. He had dark brown, coarse hair with a slight wave directly on top. He had dark eyes and even darker eyebrows that made his stare intense and captivating. He wore a mustache and, since everyone I had ever dated had been in high school, the mustache made him appear masculine, manly, and all grown up despite the dusting of freckles on his nose.

I loved his accent. Since English was his second language, he had problems sometimes with some of our words. He couldn't pronounce my name correctly and would call me Deanna which, of course, I thought sounded so much more romantic than plain old Diane. I loved learning how to speak his language—and how he'd laugh at the way my "accent" fractured the words as he asked me to try again. I loved how exotic and different he seemed from all the boys I knew. Intrigued by his culture, his habits, and his traditions, I was fascinated and I fell madly in love with him.

He was a good man—admittedly a young man barely out of his teens himself. He was a hard worker and besides working in a local factory, he was also attending school to be a mechanical engineer. He treated me with a gentleness and attention the likes of which I had never received from anyone else. I was his first love, too.

But this was just the beginning of several hard lessons to come—sometimes love just isn't enough.

Unfortunately, the differences that I first found attractive and interesting were the same ones at the root of our disagreements and problems within the relationship. We'd find ourselves arguing more and more, our different cultures and religions slowly building a wall between us. Then I found out I was pregnant.

He didn't want to be a father at this time in his life. He was also terrified of the reaction *his* father would have to the news that he had come to the United States and had gotten into trouble. Still, he offered to do the right thing.

My mother and the local parish priest arranged for us to meet at the rectory. We were given some private time to talk. My boyfriend had recently turned twenty. He offered to marry me. But he asked me to wait several months, in reality almost a year, until he turned twenty-one so he wouldn't have to face the wrath of his father.

If there hadn't already been problems surfacing between us, if the cultural differences weren't looking now like insurmountable obstacles, I might have said yes.

When I said no, I was crushed by the look of relief on his face. He couldn't get to his car fast enough to drive away. In hindsight, I don't hold that against him. He was young, scared, in a foreign country, and in big trouble.

I remember standing in the doorway of the rectory with my mother and the parish priest right behind me. I was crushed, my heart broken as I watched him drive away. I heard my mother's voice in my ear.

"Telling him no was the first mature decision you've ever made," she said.

I didn't feel mature.

I felt like running through the parking lot after him and telling him I'd changed my mind and please take me with him. Believe me, there were many times over the years I've wondered what would have happened if I had.

Now, months later, I was standing miles away in a phone booth on the boardwalk of Atlantic City, listening to my boy-friend's voice. I was in my eighth month and feeling very, very pregnant. My feet swelled if I was on them too much. I'd gained tons of weight. My back ached and it seemed the baby moved and kicked constantly.

We chitchatted briefly, if that's what you want to call it. He asked if I was okay. He asked if I was still pregnant. He knew at one time I had considered abortion, so it was a legitimate ques-tion. Then he asked me the most important question of all—why was I calling?

"Do you ever miss me?" I asked him. I didn't even realize I was holding my breath while I waited for his answer.

There was a long, uncomfortable silence.

Then he said, "Sometimes, Deanna. Sometimes."

There was nothing left to say. Those words said it all. So I simply hung up the phone. I knew I would never see or speak to him again and a deep sadness filled my being.

I sat on the beach for a long time that afternoon. I felt so alone. I wrapped my arms around my swollen belly, hugging the baby inside, and saying over and over that it would be all right. I didn't know how I'd keep that promise but, for that moment in time, I had to believe my own words to survive.

Almost four weeks later to the day, I was sitting in the dining room after lunch playing a game of 500 Rummy with Mrs. K. We'd just finished playing a hand and Mrs. K. was tallying the score when she looked up at me with a quizzical expression on her face.

"Are you feeling okay?" she asked.

"Sure. Why?"

"Well for one thing, you're not concentrating on the game. I am hundreds of points ahead of you. You've never let me get away with that big a lead."

"Game's not over yet," I replied with a grin.

"You're squirming like crazy in that chair."

I put the cards down on the table and reached my hand to the small of my back.

"My back hurts. It started last night. I thought maybe I slept the wrong way and pulled a muscle or something but it just won't go away."

Mrs. K. squinted her eyes, pursed her lips, and stared hard at me. "Does anything else hurt?"

I squirmed and shifted my position in the chair.

"Nope. Just my back. It'll go away."

"Uh huh." Mrs. K. picked up the cards, pencil, and pad and put them away. "Why don't you go upstairs and take a nap? Maybe you'll feel better when you wake up."

"Okay. I think I will. I didn't get much sleep last night."

I had just made it to the first landing of the staircase when I felt an unexpected gush. In shock, I looked down and saw pink-tinged liquid streaming down my legs and forming a puddle at my feet. My throat constricted in fear. I couldn't utter a sound. I just stared and wondered what in the world had just happened to me.

Less than a minute later that mildly annoying back pain became a strong band of pain that radiated around my waist and tightened my stomach into a ball of steel.

"Ohmigod! Ohmigod! Ohmigod!"

I found my voice as I panicked and sat down on the landing. I poked my legs through the spokes, wrapped my arms around the spokes of the railing and held on as if my life depended on it.

"Mrs. K!" I screamed.

Within seconds, Mrs. K. and several of the other girls bounded up the stairs.

"Oh my goodness, your water broke." She leaned down and put her arm around my shoulders. "Let go of the railing, Diane. You're in labor. We've got to get you to the hospital."

She might as well have been talking to a wall. The iron jaws of death wouldn't have been able to pry my arms away from the spokes of that railing. I was petrified.

Mrs. K. yelled for one of the girls to go and get my bag. In the ninth month, each of us had one packed and waiting for the "big day."

"C'mon, honey. Let go. It's going to be okay. We need to get you to the hospital."

Another band of pain, pain so intense I couldn't even cry, wrapped around my middle and squeezed so hard I finally understood firsthand what the word *agony* meant. I hung on tighter to the railing. I heard a deep, guttural moan and was surprised that I was the one making the sound.

Mrs. K. wasted no time. Within minutes, an ambulance arrived.

I guess paramedics are stronger than little old ladies in their seventies—or maybe it was because they were medical personnel and I knew they could help me—either way, they succeeded in getting me to let go.

I was strapped to a gurney and down the stairs before I realized what had happened. Mrs. K. squeezed my hand and told me everything would be all right. I remember thinking as I was wheeled beneath the landing and out the door that I was surprised the spindles of that railing were still intact.

The matrons did not accompany the girls to the hospital. They called the girls a taxi and they notified family members the girl was in labor. They notified my mother but she was several hours away and didn't come.

I spent the next three hours of my life on a stretcher in an empty room.

A nurse came in periodically, lifted the sheet, and announced how many centimeters dilated I was. I guess she was talking to me since no one else was in the room. But since I didn't have a clue what she was talking about or what a centimeter or dilation meant, nothing she said mattered— except when she said that they'd reached my doctor and he was on the way. He'd been deep sea fishing and it would be a while before he'd arrive.

So I waited.

And I writhed and squirmed and cried through every increasingly difficult labor pain.

I didn't have anyone to hold my hand or encourage me or feed me ice chips like you see on television. No one held a wet compress to my sweating forehead. No one explained the transition stage of labor and how severe but short-lived the labor pains would become.

Why should they? I didn't deserve compassion or kindness, right?

I was an unwed mother who was getting what she deserved.

I was more than afraid. I was terrified. As the pains increased to a level so severe I didn't think I could take another minute, I opened my mouth and screamed.

My body felt like I was being ripped in half.

I screamed as loudly as I possibly could and I silently prayed to die.

Then the door opened and my doctor walked in. He did a quick examination and then came up to the head of my bed. With one hand he grasped mine, with the other he smoothed some sweat-drenched hair out of my eyes and smiled down at me.

"You're doing really good. I'm proud of you. You're almost ready to deliver. I'm going to give you something to make you sleep. When you wake up, it will all be over." He nodded to the nurse. Within minutes, I slipped into blessed oblivion.

———— ❧ ————

The first sensation I remember when I woke was somebody pushing down hard on my stomach—and it hurt. I moaned and reached out a hand to stop them as I struggled to open my eyes.

"I have to do this, honey. We have to make sure you don't have any clotting problems."

Someone else steered my stretcher down the hall while the stomach-pushing nurse continued to walk beside the cart and push.

"My baby . . ." I was too groggy to say much more.

The nurse stopped pushing on my stomach for a minute and smiled. "You had a healthy baby boy."

"A boy?" A grin split my face. "Where is he? I want to see him."

The nurse who had been steering my stretcher spoke up. "We can't do that. The doctor thinks it will be easier for you if you don't see him."

Anger coursed through my body. I tried to sit up. "I want to see my baby. Please, take me to see my baby."

The stomach-pushing nurse gently lowered me back down and then glanced at the other nurse. "It can't hurt to let her have a peek. We're passing right by the nursery."

The nurse at the head of my stretcher looked like she had just sucked on a lemon. She scrunched her lips together and refrained from speaking, but soon she stopped outside a wall of windows.

The stomach-pushing nurse helped me into a sitting position and gestured to one of the nurses inside the room. Apparently, they had just finished cleaning him up and doing their measuring and weighing. He wasn't in the main nursery yet. When my nurse gestured, they brought my baby to the window. I stared at him through the glass.

He was so beautiful! And so tiny . . . and so perfect.

Tears streamed down my face. I ached to hold him in my arms. I felt overwhelmed with a wave of love like I had never experienced before in my life.

"Bring him to me."

"What?" The nurse eased me back down on the stretcher. "Honey, you know the doctor doesn't want you to do that."

"I don't care what the doctor wants. That is my baby. I want you to bring him to me."

"See?" The nurse with the pursed lips said. She resumed steering my stretcher to my room. "I knew this would be a bad idea."

No one spoke again until they had me in my room and had slid me off the stretcher and onto my bed. They started to leave.

"I want to hold my baby."

Miss Pucker Face said, "We were told you were giving this baby up for adoption."

"I am. But not today. Today he's mine and I want to hold him."

The kinder nurse came to my side. "Honey, are you sure you want to do that? It's only going to make it harder on you."

Tears continued to stream down my face. "Please . . . please bring me my son. I know I only have a couple of days with him. I understand that. But please . . . I want my baby."

The nurse nodded and stepped away.

Before she left the room, I grinned and yelled to her. "He has a name you know."

She turned in the doorway and looked back at me.

"If I had a boy, I promised myself I would name him David Brett. I looked up names and their meanings in a book. It means 'dearly beloved.' I wanted him to know that just in case someday he ever looks up his name."

I couldn't swear to it but I think that kind nurse's eyes were glistening when she nodded and left the room.

⚜

I got to spend three days with my son.

Three days that I would carry deep inside, knowing those memories would have to last a lifetime.

I fed him his bottles, burped him and changed his diapers. I cradled him in my arms and stroked the downy softness of his hair. I counted and kissed every one of his fingers and toes. I'd grin at how tightly those tiny little fingers would grasp my index finger, almost as if he would never let me go—and I'd pray that I'd find a way that maybe he'd never have to.

I'd sing him a lullaby. I'd rock him in my arms. I'd hold him tightly against my chest so he could hear the beating of my heart—that same heartbeat he had listened to for nine months.

I cried and I laughed and I smiled and I cried some more.

This was my son, my first born, and I couldn't let him go. I couldn't.

I called my mother.

"Mom, come see him. Please. He's so beautiful. He's perfect in every way. You've just got to see him."

Silence.

"He looks just like a Bradford, Mom. I can't believe how much he looks just like one of us. Won't you and Dad come see him? Please."

"Is that what you want? You haven't hurt us enough? Now you want your father to drive down there and see him? What are you trying to do? Rip out his heart?"

"But Mom . . ."

"I'm not asking your father to do that. After you sign the adoption papers, I'll bring you home."

"I'm not putting him up for adoption. I'm keeping him."

Ominous silence.

"I can't, Mom," I said in a rush, trying to fill the uncomfortable silence. "He's my son. I love him. Please . . . help me. I'll get a job. I'll find a place to live. I'll do anything but please help me keep him."

"You agreed to put him up for adoption."

"I never agreed. You're the one who's been pushing adoption for the last four months. I never wanted to do that."

More silence.

"Fine," she said. "Then keep him. But I'm done with you. You're the most selfish person I've ever met. You just don't give a damn what your actions do to other people and now you're going to ruin an innocent baby's life. I mean it, Diane. I'm done with you. Don't call here again . . . unless you come to your senses and change your mind." She slammed down the phone.

The next day, Round Two came in the form of a forty-five minute telephone call from our parish priest. The words *sin, selfishness, shame,* and *guilt* were repeated so often eventually I tuned out everything except the sound of his voice. The priest chastised me for the pain and shame I was causing my parents. Then he really lit into me for my selfishness for not putting the needs of my child before my own. He kept telling me that the child needed two loving parents, a good home, a solid religious foundation, everything I obviously couldn't provide.

The third and final round of the battle came on the third day—the last day I would ever see or hold my baby.

I had asked to see a social worker.

I was sitting in bed and holding my son in my arms when she arrived. I quickly explained my situation and asked if there was any way she could help me.

"Yes," she said. "I'll be happy to help you."

My spirits soared. At last, someone to listen to me. Someone willing to help. I would be able to keep my baby. I looked down into my son's face. I can't explain the relief and my ultimate joy.

"How are you going to help me?" I asked. "What happens next?"

"Well, we'll take the baby and put him in foster care."

"Foster care?"

"Yes. Just until you get on your feet."

"I don't understand."

"Well, you're going to need time to get established. You'll have to find a job and a place to live. You'll have to arrange for competent care to watch your son while you work." She smiled widely. "We'll take good care of your son for you while you do the things you have to do."

"Foster care?" My voice was a mere whisper as my hopes and dreams seeped out of me.

"Yes, dear. Don't worry. We have several foster families that would be willing to take him in."

I didn't have a car or a penny to my name. How was I going to find a job? I didn't have a person in the world willing to take me in until I did. How would I ever be able to do the things I needed to do before they would return my son to me? And, worse, how long would it take? Would he even be a baby anymore? Would he even recognize me as his mother?

"If I do manage to do these things, how long will it take to get my son back?"

"You must realize that it's going to take you considerable time to accomplish everything. Several months at the earliest, I'm sure. But once you're back on your feet and feel you can provide properly for your child, then our office will do an interview and an inspection. If we feel it is in the best interests of the child to return him to you, then we will petition the courts to return custody to you at that time."

Petition the courts? *They* decide the "best interests of the child"? Meanwhile, my son will be living where? In an orphanage? In a stranger's house? In more than one home?

Who would see his first tooth come in? Who would hear his first word? Who would reach out and catch him when he took his first step?

Not me.

In society at that time, most women did not yet work outside the home or have careers. Daycare centers didn't exist on every street corner like they do today. Government programs providing funds, food, and low-income housing for single moms didn't exist, or at least we weren't told about them if they did. How was I supposed to ever meet their standards and prove myself a fit mother?

At that moment, the realization finally hit me. No matter what I wanted, no matter how hard I tried, I was going to lose my baby. I knew I didn't stand a chance of ever getting him back again.

"Thank you," I said. "I'll let you know what I decide."

When the social worker left, I rocked my son in my arms. I cradled him and kissed him, all the while dying slowly each second that ticked by.

I was going to lose my son.

My only choice now was whether to give him to the social worker where his future would be uncertain and unstable or give him up for adoption where he stood a chance for stability and happiness and love.

My tears flowed so freely, a few of them actually dripped onto his beautiful little face.

My perfect child.

My first-born son.

I pressed the button for the nurse.

When they took him away for the final time, they took a piece of my soul with him. They left me with an open, aching wound that only my baby would ever be able to fill.

Numbness swept into my spirit and wrapped itself deeply around my bones. I stared out the window of my hospital room, seeing nothing, feeling nothing. I must have sat like that for hours.

When I did start to think and feel again, thoughts of my own mother crept into my mind and, for the very first time in my life, I knew what it felt like to hate.

Chapter

3

WHEN I LEFT the hospital, I didn't immediately return home. My mother had arranged for me to return to the unwed mother's home. After all, my body was different now. I needed time for the swelling of my stomach to subside. I needed time to be able to sit on a chair without using the ring cushion they'd given me at the hospital due to my stitches from the episiotomy.

You can't come home from a lucrative secretarial position in Atlantic City unless you looked the part.

I sat in a home with mothers who had not yet delivered their babies. I sat there with empty arms and an empty heart while I waited for my body to sufficiently heal so I could successfully pull off my mother's lie. I never shed a tear or spoke a word to anyone about the situation because I couldn't. I had buried the feelings so deep inside I was incapable of feeling anything at all at that time.

I did what I was supposed to do. Spoke when spoken to. Slept. Ate. Healed. Finally, I returned home.

When we pulled up to the house, my mother looked at me and said, "It's over. You have a clean slate now. Nobody has to know anything about it. So go in there and tell everyone what a good time you had in Atlantic City but you're happy to be home."

Secrets are easy to keep from outsiders, but harder to keep within families. Many of my siblings knew the truth but no one dared refute my mother's lie. So we pretended and didn't have a truthful conversation about any of it for years.

I moved back into the bedroom in a twin bed beside my younger sister and acted like I had never left. I played the game. I lived the lie. But at night I would cuddle into a fetal position in my bed and I would sob.

I started looking for a job almost immediately upon returning home. I found one as a switchboard operator for a small yarn distribution center. I had been there about two weeks when I met my future husband.

Having never operated a switchboard before, sometimes I hit the wrong buttons and accidentally disconnected people. This particularly dark, thunderstorm-filled day, Danny Flanagan was making a delivery for the boss. He was delayed because many of the roads had flooded. He made his way to a pay phone to call it in.

I disconnected him.

Three times.

On the fourth try, he yelled into the phone, "Don't hang up! I don't have any change left. Just give Mr. Orwitz a message. Let him know the roads are flooded. I'm having trouble getting back and I'll be late."

Several hours later, a very tall, very wet, very angry man appeared at my desk, dripping water from his rain gear on my switchboard and glaring at me.

"Who's the idiot who doesn't know how to answer a telephone call?" he bellowed.

My insides were shaking. I needed this job and no one knew better than I that I wasn't qualified for it and was trying to learn as I went. I lifted my eyes, brimming with tears I was determined not to shed, and said, "I'm sorry, sir. I'll try not to let it happen again."

Danny frowned at me for a minute or two and then said, "Make sure that it doesn't." Then stormed off.

It was only a few minutes later when an in-house call from the warehouse lit up on the switchboard. When I answered, Danny said, "Good. Seems you've figured out how to answer the phones inside. It's only outside ones you haven't figured out yet."

"I'm so sorry, sir."

"My name's Danny."

"I'm sorry, Danny."

"You can make it up to me by apologizing to me again over lunch. What do you say?"

I smiled. "Sure. Lunch would be fine."

We went out to lunch, no place fancy, a little diner not far from work. Then he'd start finding excuses to walk by my desk several times a day. Then he'd start taking his coffee break the same time I did.

He was a tall man with a good sense of humor. He had dark hair and wore a dark mustache—similar to my past boyfriend. He drove the exact same model car down to the year and color that my baby's father had driven. I hadn't consciously noticed those similarities. But my mother did.

When he pulled up to my house to take me on a date, we'd known each other about a week. I can still remember the look of shock on my mother's face when she saw him walk down our driveway.

"Are you kidding me?" she asked.

I didn't understand the question at the time. I truly did not see those similarities and I thought maybe she just didn't like him or think he was good-looking enough or rich enough or whatever. I didn't ask Mom for her opinions anymore.

We went out and, later that night, he did what most guys do: he made a pass. I turned him down. I burst into tears and blurted out where I'd been for the past five months and why.

Nothing makes a man scoot across a car seat and put his hands back on the wheel faster than an announcement like that one.

But Danny was nice. He didn't end the date. He asked me questions. And more important than anything, he listened. He just sat and listened as I told him all about this perfect little baby boy who I had just lost.

We saw each other almost every night for the next week. We'd drive somewhere. He'd pull over. I'd talk. He'd listen. I was so grateful for his kindness, for the chance to tell another human being how much I missed my son. I was so desperate to feel that someone genuinely cared about me that I convinced myself that I was falling in love.

I was so emotionally and psychologically messed up at the time that I was incapable of loving anyone but, of course, I didn't realize it.

One day I came home from work and found my mother waiting at the door for me. I could tell from the angry expression on her face that she was upset about something and I wondered what I had done now. When I reached the door, she said, "Come with me."

We walked downstairs and I followed her into the laundry room.

"What's wrong?" I asked.

"This came in the mail today." She handed me a letter that had obviously been addressed to me but she had felt at total liberty to open. I took the letter from her hand and began to read.

It was from the adoption agency. It told me that the adoptive parents lived in New Jersey but didn't tell me where, that the father was a mechanical engineer and the mother was an English teacher, that they had tried for five years to have a child of their own and that they were thrilled with the addition of Brett to their family.

Those all-familiar tears filled my eyes.

Brett. They'd dropped the name David, but at least they'd kept part of his name.

A mechanical engineer. Wow! That's what his biological father was studying to be.

An English teacher. I'd considered becoming an English teacher once.

I didn't know these parents and never would, but they sounded hand-picked by God.

My mother ripped the letter out of my hand. She held it over an ash tray sitting on the washing machine lid, lit the bottom right corner of the letter with her cigarette lighter, and both of us watched it burn until it was nothing more than gray ashes.

My mother looked at me. "We will never talk about this again." Then she walked out of the room and up the stairs.

Never talk about it again? Is that how you got rid of pain and loss and grief? Is that how you disposed of your first-born grandchild? My son? Just torch all the evidence that he ever existed with a cigarette lighter?

One week later, I ran off and eloped with Danny.

We were living in a room in the Deer Trail Inn when, because of the overtime hours Danny worked, he asked me to find us an apartment, so I did.

In those days, people were more naïve. We didn't have computers, Internet, cell phones. The television shows we watched were *I Love Lucy* and *The Dick Van Dyke Show*, on which married couples dressed in chaste pajamas and slept in twin beds. Children played outside and not with video games. It was a different world back then. We were sheltered. We were naïve. I was a grown woman chronologically but, at that time, I probably had the maturation age of a fifteen-year-old. I was used to my parents making all the decisions and had never learned how to use good judgment or make good decisions on my own.

So when Danny asked me to go shopping for an apartment, I was excited and eager to do it.

I had found a two bedroom, one floor walk-up apartment above a storefront in downtown Paterson that was priced well within our budget and made an appointment to see it. I went after work. It was dark and the landlord told me the electricity wouldn't be turned on until he had a paying tenant. He showed me the apartment by the glow of his cigarette lighter.

Yeah, I know. I'm cringing, too, admitting my stupidity.

We walked through the rooms and I knew they were large, particularly the kitchen, but I really couldn't see much with such little light. I was hesitating and planned on coming back with Dan when two other people walked in. The man showed the apartment to this woman the same way. The only difference was this woman ooh-ed and ahh-ed in each room and said she wanted it and was ready to give a deposit and sign the lease on the spot.

My guy said, "No, you don't. We were here first and this lady has first rights to the place." Then he told me he couldn't hold it and I had to sign now or it would go to the other woman.

I gave him our money and signed the lease.

Stupid! Stupid! Stupid!

When I brought Danny the next day in daylight to see our new home, I couldn't believe my eyes. The place was filthy. It was so dirty, there was a black grease stain from floor-to-ceiling where an old pot-bellied stove had once been and the flue at the top had been sloppily filled in with cement. Roaches ran rampant. The bedroom windows were warped and wouldn't close all the way.

I will never forget the look of horror on Danny's face.

"I'll fix it!" I promised. "I'll have it sparkling clean by the time you get home tonight."

He was angry, and I can't say I blame him. He shook his head and headed out for work. Before he left, I asked him what was his favorite color? He said, "Purple."

When Dan got home at ten p.m. that night, I had scrubbed the place the best I could. I had a pink sofa and blue chair delivered from Salvation Army for our first living room set. And I had painted every room in the apartment a different shade of purple!

Danny never liked that color again.

The months after I married Danny Flanagan passed in a blur. We had married exactly twenty-one days from the day we met. I didn't know the man, and he didn't know me. Looking back on it years later, it wasn't a big surprise to either of us that the marriage was not based on love and did not have a good foundation for all the trials and tribulations that all marriages experience.

I wanted to get away from my mother. I wanted to run away from never-ending pain. I wanted to believe somebody, anybody, in this world thought that I was worth loving.

Danny had his own reasons for marrying me. He felt sorry for me and genuinely wanted to help me. He also, unbeknownst to me at the time, was a convicted felon who had just served time for armed robbery. He was on a methadone maintenance program because he was a recovering heroin addict. He married me thinking it would be his clean slate, an opportunity to live a whole new life.

Of course, this information about him never came into the conversation in the twenty-one days I knew him.

He continued to hide the information from me for many months. I only knew him as a warehouse worker who put in tons of overtime. I was stupid, naïve, immature. I accepted without question his excuse that we couldn't ride to work together because he was working overtime. I never suspected it was because he was reporting to a clinic for his daily dose of methadone and he didn't want me or anyone at work to know.

But decades later, life has taught me at least one very valuable lesson: in time, everything is revealed. That's what makes lying so insidious. Eventually, the truth comes out every time.

Danny wasn't satisfied with methadone. He began to wash it down with alcohol. It wasn't long before I realized I was married to an active alcoholic. Dealing with that reality for a twenty-year-old was hard enough. I was ill equipped to cope with my own emotional issues let alone know how to deal with alcoholism.

Gradually, over six months or so, the rest of his secrets came to light, as well.

I panicked when I found out I was married to an active alcoholic, drug-addicted felon. I was also pregnant.

I called my mother and begged to come home.

The homecoming was tense, to say the least. I give my mother credit. From her point of view, I was the selfish, ungrateful child she kept trying to help, the one who kept defying her, who kept making messes that she was expected to clean up. I'm not sure, if I had been the mother and received that telephone call, that I would have opened the door again. I was grateful to her. I truly was.

For the time we were back together, I honestly tried to be the daughter she wanted. I was polite and grateful and obedient. If she said "jump," I was more than willing to say, "Sure, Mom, how high?" I was home. (Although, this was Michigan now, not New Jersey.) But home isn't lumber and a roof. It is family, so I was home.

I was surrounded by my siblings and, again, sharing a room with one of my kid sisters. I was content and happy and eagerly looking forward to the birth of my child seven months from then. I even made an appointment at the local college with a counselor for career advice. I brought home brochures to my parents and the three of us began to talk about viable careers, what evening classes I could take, and what job I might be able to handle while I went to school.

Life was good.

I admit that I selfishly wondered why they couldn't have been this helpful with the birth of my first child. Did legitimacy really make that much difference to my parents? Did a marriage certificate, a mere piece of paper, really change the love a grandparent can feel for a child?

But I had been such a wild child; I knew better than to voice these feelings. I worked hard to push any negative feelings about the adoption last year into the deep recesses of my soul. My parents were helping me now and I was so, so grateful. I was going to make my mother proud of me. I was going to make her happy that she'd decided to give me another chance.

That plan lasted a total of ten days.

My mother and I went out for the day shopping. We had had a very pleasant morning and both of us, tired and ready for lunch, decided to hit a local garage sale we were passing. We parked the car and had separated briefly since we were looking for different items when my eyes fell on a tiny, little dress.

I picked up the little piece of fluff and lace. A quick glance at the tag showed it was meant for a newborn. I played with the pink ribbon and smoothed the satin and lace. Should I buy it? I didn't know whether I'd have a girl or a boy so purchasing clothing seemed a foolish waste of money.

But this was a garage sale. The amount they were asking for the dress was equivalent to what I'd pay for a can of soda. I was still contemplating whether it was a frivolous decision when my mother walked up behind me.

"Look," I said, smiling widely and holding up the tiny dress. "Isn't it beautiful? Should I buy it? I've got a fifty-fifty chance I'll have a girl. What do you think?"

"What are you buying baby clothes for?" My mother had a puzzled expression on her face. "You're not keeping this child. You're putting it up for adoption."

I will never be able to put into words the feelings that rushed through me. I was in total shock. I felt like I'd been run over by a truck and now the truck was going to back up and run over me again.

"What?" I could barely squeeze the word out in a whisper.

"We'll put it up for adoption. There's no way you will be able to handle college and a job with a baby. This will give you a clean slate." Her eyes narrowed and her tone of voice became ominous. "And this time you will do what I say when I say it. Is that understood? No more screwing up. This is your last chance."

"But I'm married." I know that was a stupid thing to whisper. I don't know what I was thinking. Probably that being married made the pregnancy acceptable. Never in my wildest dreams when I sat at the dining room table with my parents, discussing college plans and jobs, did I realize that my baby was not part of those plans.

"That's why you can stay home this time. We'll tell everyone that you're a widow and that your husband was killed in Vietnam."

Widow?

Of course, how could I be so stupid? In those days being an unwed mother was the greatest sin you could commit. The second biggest shame was being divorced. Society hadn't progressed to the multiple marriages and divorces prevalent today.

I lost it.

I yelled at my mother. Right there. In public. In front of a small crowd of gaping strangers.

"What's wrong with you? Are you crazy? What do you think I am, a %#@*#* baby machine? I just crank out kids and give them away to other women?"

I placed my hands on my stomach almost protectively.

"You are *not* taking this baby away from me. No one is ever going to take this baby away from me."

I started walking toward the car, but had to throw in one more angry and cruel jab. I glanced over my shoulder and yelled, "You need help! Something's wrong with a mother who can't love her own children or grandchildren."

I am not proud of my behavior or of the mean, cruel, thoughtless things I said to my mother. She was trying in her own confused, twisted way to help me. She honestly didn't understand why giving this child away and getting a chance to go to college and have a career, the things she'd dreamed about and would never have the chance to do, would not be welcomed by me.

I hurt her. I was disrespectful and cruel. I never apologized to my mother but I didn't purposely try not to. Throughout the years, the incident became just one more thing I buried inside. One more thing we didn't speak about. One more thing we pretended hadn't happened.

It wasn't until I started writing this book that my emotions and memories of those situations came to the surface again. I wish I had apologized to my mother. I wish we had had a chance as adults to sit down and discuss this terribly painful, traumatic time in our lives. I wasn't the only one impacted by the decision to place my first born up for adoption. My mother was, too. I believe my mother second-guessed the wisdom of her decisions and, maybe in her own way, even grieved the loss of her first grandchild.

Somehow, I truly hope the good Lord has let my mother read these pages. I hope she knows that I'm sorry and that I wish I had been a better daughter. I wish I had handled things in a more mature, loving way. I hope the Lord lets her know that I understand. I really do. I forgive her . . . and I hope in her lifetime she was able to forgive me.

We make decisions in our lives, sometimes foolish ones, sometimes damaging ones, but we always make those decisions with good intentions. We don't set out to hurt people. We don't set out to cause ripples in a stream that become tsunamis of destruction. We take children to doctors for medical needs but frequently don't take our children for psychological help—or we do and then are blamed later in life for that decision, too.

Life is nothing but choices and every choice ripples out and touches and transforms, for better or worse, everyone else in our lives.

As I said earlier, my mother did the best she could as the person she was, dealing with the circumstances she faced.

And so did I.

Within twenty-four hours of our argument at the garage sale, I was on a plane flying back to my drug-addicted, alcoholic, felon husband. No one was going to be able to take my baby away. I was going to find a way to get my husband off drugs and alcohol. I was determined to mold him into a good husband and father even if it killed me. And it almost did.

Chapter

4

THE FIRST ORDER of business when I arrived back in New Jersey was to figure out a way to pick up the pieces of my life. I confronted my husband, who was coming off a drunken bender and had a hangover to beat all hangovers, and gave him an ultimatum. I told him he had a chance to be a better man. That we were expecting a child who would need two parents—two sober, hard-working, loving parents—and I wanted us to be those parents. I told him I would help him keep sober and drug free. That I wanted our marriage to work and I was willing to do anything to make sure it did.

But I also told him that I would not allow my children to grow up in an atmosphere of alcohol and drugs. That he had to get his act together or we were done. I'd divorce him and I'd do it on my own.

I gave him the choice. Do you want to be a father to your child? Or do you want to continue to spend your life in alcoholic stupors?

He chose us.

I was surprised and happy. We would find a way to make it work. We'd become a family. Family is all I ever wanted.

The first order of business was getting him off the methadone maintenance program and into a rehab center. That wasn't an easy task. He decided to go cold turkey and kick methadone. He shouldn't have. He was horribly sick for days. I placed blankets on top of him as his body trembled with chills. I watched him twist into a fetal position with stomach cramps. I listened to him groan in pain. I moved aside as he ran to the bathroom, barely able to control the contents of his stomach in either direction.

It took a good week, but he did it.

I was so proud of him and so hopeful for the future.

We got him into a rehab in Princeton. It was on the grounds of a mental hospital and allowed no visitors. Unfortunately, his placement in the rehab also resulted in me being homeless. Literally. I had nowhere to go. We'd moved out of that dive of an apartment months ago. We had been staying in a room over a bar. With Danny gone, so was the room and the money. I now had no roof over my head. No friends or family I could ask for help. Those bridges were burned. I had one apple to my name and some loose change.

I ate my apple and tried to figure out what to do next. I was in downtown Trenton, walking the streets. My husband was going to be away for a couple of months. I was five months pregnant and I knew I couldn't remain on the streets.

I'd seen a billboard advertising a company called Birth-Right, which was a non-profit organization that offered alternative solutions to pregnant mothers other than abortion—even married ones. When I called and explained my situation, I was given help immediately.

I was placed with a groundskeeper, Hank, his wife, Dee, and their seven children. Hank took care of a huge piece of property owned by the Catholic Church. The estate house on the property was a retirement home for nuns. As part of his salary, his family lived in the chauffeur's cottage. As the years passed and more and more children came along, the garages had been converted into bedrooms and adjoined the cottage. In return for my room and board, I did chores and helped in the main kitchen two weekends a month when the church ran Marriage Encounter weekends for couples.

That family changed my life. They were the kindest, most compassionate people I had ever met. I was good friends with all of them but became particularly close to the wife, Dee. She remained my best friend for fifteen years. She died in her forties of ovarian cancer. I miss her to this day. Being the oldest of seven children myself, when I moved in with this large family, it felt like I was living at home. And yet . . . it was nothing like my home. This mother and father were very hands-on with their children. They showered them with love and affection as well as discipline and direction. They showed genuine interest in what was going on in their lives and who their friends were. Their basketball hoop in the driveway was a frequent haunt by local kids on weekends followed by barbeques and board games shared by friends and family alike.

These children were taught the importance of developing a work ethic. They had daily chores, even the youngest four-year-old. I remember being amazed that the dinner plates were stored in the lower cabinets so the littlest ones would be able to set the table for meals.

They raised chickens, collected eggs, tended a huge garden, canned vegetables and fruit in mason jars for the winter. They started their day with prayers, said prayers at each meal, and ended their days with prayer. The children were respectful and loving and obedient. They were involved in scouts and every one of them took on some form of community service.

I remember one particular Thanksgiving years later, Dee and I and a group of other women worked together cooking a full-course meal for the local migrant workers. The men drove out to the farms and gathered the migrant families together and brought them to our location. All the children, ours and the migrant workers, played together, and I remember watching my three-year-old son, Dan, dancing on the stage with the other kids and having the time of his life.

Living for those few months with this family didn't change me overnight. It took many, many more years before the Lord finally got attention from me that was long overdue. But those years with that family did start me on my journey and impacted my life in a million different ways. Part of who I am today comes from my experiences with that family, witnessing the love they had for each other and the love they bestowed on others. I saw a family that didn't just say they believed in God; they showed it in their actions every day of their lives.

Hank and Dee made connections within the community with some of the priests they knew. When Danny was released from rehab, one of the priests had arranged an interview for Danny with a local steel company where he got a decent job. The priest also helped us get an apartment.

The transition to our apartment and married life was bumpy at best. Danny was off drugs but he couldn't seem to kick the alcohol. I'll give him credit for trying. He'd go weeks without a drink but inevitably he'd slip again . . . and again . . . and again.

I kept doing all the wrong things. I kept nagging, fighting, complaining, threatening, covering up for him, bailing him out—enabling him—which resulted in the very opposite of what I wanted to achieve.

There was one particular incident from those early days that has stuck in my memory and just won't go away. When I was eight-and-a-half months pregnant with my son, Dan, I got a call from the police that my husband and a semi-truck driver got into a road rage incident on the highway. They got out of their vehicles and had a physical confrontation. The truck driver smashed a crow bar into Danny's head. Both men were currently at the police station.

When I arrived at the police station, I found that both men had apologized, refused to press charges against each other, and left. So I drove home expecting to find Danny there. Not only was he *not* there, but he and the truck driver had gone out drinking together. The next telephone call came in the wee hours of the night when the hospital called and told me that Danny had been admitted with a concussion—after the bars closed, of course.

The day Danny was released from the hospital, I was admitted. My blood pressure was soaring and the doctor's feared toxemia. A couple days later, they induced labor. I tried calling Danny several times to let him know I would be delivering that day but couldn't reach him. My only other idea was to call my sister-in-law, Marie, to see if she could somehow get in touch with him. She took over the calls for me. She finally reached him. He had gone out drinking the night before and was in such a deep sleep, he never heard the phone. She got him to the hospital.

But not in time.

For the second time in my life, I went through labor and delivery alone.

Even though this time I was awake through the whole process and had had a natural childbirth without drugs, I wasn't allowed to see or hold my baby. He was born blue and instantly whisked away to the neonatal care unit.

It was hours before they would let me out of bed to go down to the nursery. They told me that I still couldn't hold him but that I could see him through the glass. They placed my wheelchair as close to the glass as they could and I saw my son for the first time.

He had jet black hair and narrowed eyes that gave him an almost Asian appearance. He was beautiful and perfect—and this child didn't look like me or any of my family members at all. He was 100 percent his father's son. He was lying in an incubator with lights shining on him and he was the largest baby in the nursery!

All the other infants in the NICU were so tiny. Two, three, four pounds. Dan weighed in at nine pounds, two ounces. Compared to the other babies, he was huge. The nurse and I chuckled at his size. She told me I couldn't come in or hold him yet but she didn't think it would be much longer.

It took another twenty-four hours before they determined there was nothing seriously wrong with him and the blueness had simply been because he was cold. They took him out of the NIC unit and brought him to me.

I was overcome with joy. He was almost the size and feel of a two- or three-month-old. I didn't even have to stabilize his neck because his muscles were strong enough that he was already trying to raise it and look at me. He was alert and attentive and held his head still when I spoke to him, like he was really trying to listen to every word.

I basked in the joy all new mothers feel. I counted his fingers and toes. I kissed his head and his hands and his feet. I cradled him in my arms and continued to be amazed at how much hair he had and how thick and dark it was.

Danny had seen his son through the glass windows but had not yet had the opportunity to hold him. He hadn't arrived yet that day and, for this short period of time, it was just my baby and me. I will never forget those precious moments. The feelings were almost overwhelming. I had gone through so much to keep him and now he was here in my arms where prior to this moment he had only been in my heart.

I was happy beyond belief and so deeply in love with this pudgy little boy, who looked nothing like me but was still mine. My smile was so wide, my face hurt.

But there was no way I could hold this child and not remember my other son. My tiny little guy with wispy light hair. The baby who looked just like me and my family. My first-born son, who I would never be able to hold in my arms again.

The agony and the ecstasy. Total joy. Total pain. And I felt them both.

When my son, Dan, was born, my best friend, Dee, was one of the first to hold him. Her children stood up as godparents for my siblings who couldn't be there. My family didn't see Dan until he was about two months old—when I left Danny for the second time.

Danny always managed to hold a job despite his alcoholism. But there were many payday weekends when he'd disappear on a Friday and not show up until Sunday night with empty pockets. Somehow, we always managed to scrape together enough money to pay the rent so we'd have a roof over our heads. Everyone and everything else had to stand in line and sometimes the line got pretty long.

Of course, his frequent weekend jaunts led to brutal verbal arguments. Danny would straighten out for a few weeks. But eventually, he'd slip and I'd live through another weekend of not knowing where he was, who he was with, or even if he would return.

Again, I contacted my parents. Again, my parents allowed me to move back home.

This time was different. This time my mother had converted a bedroom to a bedroom/nursery for me, complete with my twin bed, a baby crib, and a rocking chair. She was kind to me and seemed to accept the situation for what it was.

Danny sent child support regularly. I took every babysitting job I could get my hands on to supplement the money I was giving my parents for our support. I even started house sitting/babysitting for parents who wanted a weekend or even a week away. As long as I could bring my child with me, it worked and worked well.

I was happy. My parents seemed accepting. My siblings, mere children themselves, played with Dan and treated him as if he was just another one of the clan.

Of course, there were nights when I'd glance over at my son asleep in his crib and I'd wonder about the child I gave away. My heart would ache a deep, awful hurt that never completely went away. I couldn't help but wonder who was holding my baby in their arms? Who was watching him sleep in his crib?

I'd push those feelings down into that dark dungeon inside me. I had to in order to survive, to be any kind of a loving mother for this little one. I prayed that God was watching over my lost baby, the baby my arms still ached to hold. I said prayers of thanksgiving for this little dark-haired infant asleep beside me. And I went on with my life.

The deal I made with my husband at the beginning of the summer was that he had to stop drinking permanently. He had to go to AA. He had to send weekly support checks. And if he did, if he could stay sober, attend meetings, and keep up with his financial obligations, then I would return. I gave him four months to do it.

I never believed he would be able to meet those demands. I felt comfortable planning a future with my family and contemplating a divorce from my husband. It was sad, but I almost wished he *wouldn't* meet the demands. I didn't love him.

He didn't love me. I didn't want to go back. I just wanted to be with my family and raise my son.

But Danny called every Saturday. He sent a check weekly. He told both me and my parents he was working hard to turn his life around, attending meetings, saving for the down payment on a doublewide mobile home.

At the end of the four month separation, he asked the inevitable. He asked me to come home.

My mother and I sat at the kitchen table and talked about it. I told her that I didn't love the man and that I didn't want to go back. I told her I wanted to stay in Michigan and that I'd do anything she'd ask of me if she would help me stay.

"No, Diane, you can't." Her tone wasn't angry or mean. Truthfully, she looked sad. "You made your choice when you married this man. He's your child's father. He's done everything you asked him to do. You made a deal with him and he kept his end of the bargain. Now you have to do the same."

"I don't want to go back, Mom. Please don't make me."

"Your son deserves a home with two parents who love him. I know Danny has had problems in the past but I've talked to him many times over the summer. I believe he truly loves his son. I also believe he is working very hard to get things right. You owe him a second chance, Diane. You have to go back."

We rented a small moving van and a couple of my brothers drove me all the way back from Michigan to Pennsylvania. I didn't say much during the trip. My mother was right. I had to grow up and face responsibility for the choices I had made. I was a married woman with a child and I didn't belong in my mother's upstairs bedroom. I had had a wonderful summer surrounded by family and filled with love. But it was time now to grow up and leave.

When we arrived at the apartment, Danny was thrilled to see us. He immediately took the baby from my arms. "I can't believe how much he looks like me." He kissed him and held him and talked to him.

Maybe it was going to be okay.

It didn't take long to unpack the van. I didn't have many things. Then my brothers hugged me and left for home.

They hadn't been gone more than a couple of hours when Danny hit me with the news. He hadn't been going to meetings. He'd lied. He'd been drinking . . . a lot. He hadn't paid the rent for a couple of months and we were going to be evicted.

Welcome home.

I didn't call and tell my parents. When I came back this time, I finally realized that my life was *my* life, filled with obligations and responsibilities, and I couldn't keep running home to my parents. Not anymore.

I'd made a series of bad choices. Those choices had consequences. I'd have to find a way to deal with those consequences.

And I did.

It took a while. We borrowed money from Hank and Dee to pay the back rent. Danny found a second job and worked hard to pay them back every cent.

He started attending AA meetings and I knew he wasn't lying to me this time because I drove him to them. We moved to another apartment and began to save money for a doublewide mobile home in a family park.

Life became routine, stable, and for the very first time, I actually had hope that everything was going to be all right.

———— ༄ ————

Everything changed the Christmas before my third child was born. I was six months pregnant. It was Christmas Eve, a Friday night, and Danny didn't come home.

I knew there would have probably been a Christmas party after work and I'd hoped that he'd skip it. He didn't.

I was at my wit's end. He couldn't be doing this to us on Christmas, could he?

I was angry and hurt and fed up. I'd promised myself that I would never let my children see their father drunk. So far, I'd kept that promise, but Dan was almost three and the child I carried was only a few months away. I wouldn't be able to hide their father's drinking from them much longer.

It was after midnight, Christmas Day for all intents and purposes, when the police called. Danny was at the station. He'd been arrested for a DUI. He had gone before the night judge, had been put on probation with mandatory AA attendance, and was released on his own recognizance. The police needed me to come to the station and drive him home.

Merry Christmas.

I didn't realize it at the time, but that incident had truly been the best Christmas gift I ever received. The probation officer kept a close watch on Danny, made sure he made his meetings, made sure he kept sober and kept his job. The courts did something that a nagging, constantly complaining wife had been unable to do—they put him on a path that kept him clean and sober for almost *seven years*.

Those seven years were good years.

We moved from the apartment to a doublewide mobile and then two years later we moved into a large, three-bedroom townhouse in a really nice neighborhood.

We gave our children the life I had always dreamed for them. Our home backed up to Five Mile Woods, a government-owned property. My two boys went on many a hike and had adventures with their friends in those woods. We had an above-ground pool in our backyard, making our home a favorite haunt for the neighbors and their children on hot summer afternoons.

We threw parties and hosted neighborhood barbeques. We had season tickets to Great Adventure amusement park and went there frequently, not only to ride the rides, but to see the shows. We went to the beach in the summer. We even took a neighborhood family white-water rafting trip down the Lehigh River.

We lived on a cul-de-sac. Because it was a new neighborhood, most of us moved in around the same time. We were a group of young couples enjoying the excitement of owning our first homes. We had young children very close in age and the children made fast friends and grew up together.

Danny and I still weren't madly in love with one another. But it didn't matter. We liked one another. We liked one another enough to provide the home we wanted for our family. We loved our children with a passion. The only thing important to either one of us was our family. So we made it work.

Yes, life was good.

Unbeknownst to me, there was another cul-de-sac eight miles away across the bridge in New Jersey. That cul-de-sac was in a quiet neighborhood composed mainly of working and older adults. Two families on this cul-de-sac each had a son close in age. The boys played together almost every day—until the one boy moved away.

Because there weren't any other children on this street, the boy left behind spent the next eight years of his life alone. As a little boy, he played with his Legos and Matchbox cars. When he got a bit older, he set up a wooden board to throw balls against. He'd practice his pitch in an attempt to excel in the game of baseball which he loved.

He became used to being alone. He became used to making his own decisions, thinking his own thoughts, entertaining himself. He wasn't unhappy. He came to like his own company. It built self-confidence and a self-trust that maybe he wouldn't have formed any other way.

He was an adopted boy, living eight miles away from the door of his birth mother, and neither one of them ever knew it.

Chapter

5

Steve

I found out I was adopted when I was young, six or seven, maybe?

I don't remember a lot about the whole thing. Who remembers that age?

I was a kid.

It was the Seventies. I lived with my parents in a middle-class neighborhood on a quiet cul-de-sac. I was the only kid on that block. When I wasn't in school, my world consisted of playing with Matchbox® cars and building cool things with blocks.

If somebody asked *you* what your life was like at six or what you could remember, I'd bet you'd have a hard time thinking of anything special, too. Especially if you were a normal kid, with normal parents, living a happy life—and it was a happy life.

My parents were good parents. I had everything I needed and more. Birthdays around my house were more like Christmas. And Christmas, well I probably had the best ones any kid could have.

Yeah, I had a regular, normal, happy kid's life.

So I don't remember specifics.

But I do remember where and how I found out I was adopted.

My parents were away for the weekend on some kind of trip and my grandmother was looking out for me. This part I remember pretty well.

I was in the bathtub when my grandmother said, "Your mother isn't your real mother."

I don't remember why she said it. Don't remember if I said something or did something that made her say it. I just remember the words.

"Your mother isn't your *real* mother."

Sure, she was. What was with Grandmom?

I was confused. I know I didn't comprehend the importance of the words she'd just said. But they bothered me enough to tuck them away in my head. They bothered me enough to be able to look back on that time in my life and remember that day and what I was doing and who I was with.

Those words changed my life. I just didn't know how much at the time.

I remember my mother's reaction when I told her.

It was a couple days later and my mother was standing at the kitchen sink when I asked, "Mom, what did Grandmom mean when she said you're not my real mother?"

She turned and looked at me. "What did she say?"

I could tell from the tone in her voice and her slow, deliberate movements that this was a pretty big deal. I just hoped I wasn't going to get in trouble for any of it.

"Grandmom said you're not my real mom."

I don't remember my mother's answer. Whatever she said must have satisfied my curiosity.

I do remember arguing—lots and lots of arguing—between my mother and grandmother and dad. Seemed everybody was mad at each other for a very long time.

I'm fuzzy on the details. I do remember Dad wanted me to apologize to my grandmother, but I honestly can't remember why. I guess I must have said something that triggered the conversation that caused the blow-up. Who knows?

When writing this memoir together, my biological mother asked me tons of questions. What did your adoptive parents say? How did they explain it? How did you feel?

I was a kid!

I was fine with it. I blew it off as nothing. I was a happy kid. I had a happy life.

It wasn't until my teenage years that I started to think about it.

Yeah, it was my teenage years when I started to think about it more and more.

Diane

One of the lessons I've learned about life is that many things are cyclical. Bad times become good times if you wait long enough. And, unfortunately, since heaven doesn't exist on this planet, good times can slip back into bad.

I didn't understand that many men when they reach their forties go through a mid-life crisis. They start to think about their own mortality and don't like the thoughts. They start to wonder what they can do to feel young again, to ward off the passage of time.

I didn't really believe that such a thing existed. It seemed the subject made good fodder for talk shows and magazine articles but was no more real than the latest sighting of Bigfoot.

But I was wrong.

Sometimes the crisis is more a bump-in-the-road rather than a full-blown disaster. It might appear as a husband taking on a hobby he'd never shown an interest in before, like deep sea fishing or skeet shooting, when the most exciting thing he'd ever done before in his life was swig a beer by the backyard barbeque grill.

He'd do something that appeared absolutely normal and millions of other men already did—something he'd never done. Maybe a man would buy a fancy sports car and then collect tickets racing it over the speed limit on major highways. Some men bought motorcycles complete with leather jackets and hit the open roads on weekends. Some took up photography or picked up an instrument, got together with a couple male friends and started a garage band.

Normal things. Innocent things that cause nothing more than a bump or blip in the marriage.

But sometimes the crisis is actually a crisis. It creeps up slowly and hits you with one major change after another until neither one of you know exactly how you got to this place in your lives . . . or how to survive it.

Our crisis began when my husband, Danny, came home from work one day and announced we were going to sell our house and move to the Jersey shore.

I don't know what came as more of a surprise—that my husband wanted to sell a house we both loved and move away from all our friends or that he wanted to move to the shore which, of course, struck me as extremely odd since he hated the salt water, the sandy beach, and anything and everything shore related.

But I loved the shore. It had been one of the good memories from my childhood.

Vacations are expensive. My parents had seven children and the only vacations they could afford would be annual trips to visit my uncle in Absecon, New Jersey, or occasionally visit my grandmother in Ocean City, Maryland. As a kid, some of the happiest memories of my life were the summers we spent in Brigantine on the beach. And despite my husband's disdain for the shore, I made certain my children made many trips to the beach.

So when my husband came up with the brilliant idea to sell our home and move to the shore, he didn't find opposition from me. I wondered why he wanted to make the move, of course. I raised an eyebrow or two and questioned him about the decision several times before we actually went through with it. He just kept telling me he wanted to make a change and that I was right and it would be a good thing to raise the children by the beach. Eventually, I agreed.

It was another one of my huge mistakes.

We found a home in Lanoka Harbor north of Atlantic City and just south of Toms River. It was minutes from the beach and had a large in-ground pool in the backyard, twice the size of our little above-ground.

I got a job as a secretary for the public relations director at the Toms River hospital. I loved my job particularly for its diversity. One day I might be helping my boss plan a high-society fundraising dinner and on another day I might be escorting a Michael Jackson impersonator through the hospital to visit the children's ward.

Danny, believe it or not, continued to commute an hour and a half from his job outside Trenton to our new home.

I thought everything was great. Everyone was happy.

I thought wrong.

Even when Danny began dieting and losing a lot of weight, when he changed his hair style . . . even when he traded his comfortable flannel shirts for sport shirts and nice jeans, I didn't realize trouble was brewing.

I'd compliment him on the changes in his appearance. I can remember one instance, in particular, when I actually came up behind him while he was standing at the coffee pot getting a cup of brew. I wrapped my arms around his waist, placed my head on his back, and said, "Wow! You're looking so good these days. I better be careful or some sweet young thing is going to come along and snatch you away."

Both of us laughed. Little did we know.

Shortly after we moved to the Lanoka Harbor home, my sister called. She was going through a difficult divorce and, due to extenuating family circumstances, it wasn't a good idea for her to move in with my parents. She needed a place to stay and, of course, Danny and I welcomed her with open arms to our home.

She moved in with her two children—a girl, aged four, and a little boy, aged two. We only had three bedrooms so we turned our formal dining room into a fourth bedroom. It was a small home and now it became smaller. But isn't that what families do? They reach out and help one another when it's needed. So our two families merged into one within the walls of my little shore home.

For months we thought we had the perfect situation. I'd work during the day. She'd work as a waitress at night. All four children were cared for and never left alone.

The trouble started when I switched from the day shift to a more lucrative position on the night shift in the nursing department and my sister switched from nights to days at the restaurant.

To this day, I will never truly understand what happened or how it happened. All I know is less than six months after my sister walked in my door, my husband stared me right in the eyes and declared his undying love—for my sister.

Before I ever knew what hit me, I had filed for divorce, had moved with my children back to Michigan to live with my parents, and was unsuccessfully trying to cope with more of life's hurts, betrayals, and pain.

My sister was living with her children in *my* home with *my* husband who was now the new love in *her* life.

I've reconciled with my sister since those days. It wasn't easy and took many, many years to get past the betrayal and hurt. To this day, I do not know, and probably never will know, why she did what she did. Truthfully, even now, over three decades later, I don't believe she knows what made her make the choices she made either.

All I will say in her defense is that our childhood home held more secrets than are shared here. Secrets that hurt. Secrets that scar. Possibly those secrets could cause a person to be so afraid of going back that they kick into their own survival mode and do whatever they have to not to return.

My sister caused me and my children unbearable pain and negatively impacted our lives. That's the truth.

But I can't and won't judge her. People aren't perfect. Imperfect people can do terrible, horrible things to each other and yet still be worth loving and forgiving.

My sister is one of those people.

I love her. I forgave her.

She has to live with the consequences of what she did and, when I look back at her life since those days, she has paid and continues to pay for her choices.

Needless to say, the divorce was not amicable.

Divorces are never easy on the children, but ours was extra difficult.

My children's aunt now took on the role of their step-mother. Their cousins, living in their old house, now called my children's father Dad. The familial emotional support most people rely on when they divorce—support of parents, siblings, aunts, and uncles—was now torn between two sisters. No one thought what my sister did was right. But they loved her as well as me.

She was our sister. The situation became a nightmare for everyone, particularly the children.

Add into the mix a father who didn't care what he was doing to his boys, who only cared about how good it felt to be with a new, younger woman. Then add a mother who fell into a depression so deep she was barely able to crawl out of bed at the start of each day or function on any level at all, and you'll understand why my children didn't stand a chance.

The divorce messed them up. Danny and I messed them up. Their fun-loving childhood innocence disappeared overnight and their teenage years were filled with pain, confusion, and acting out.

In his teens, my youngest son, David Mark, turned to alcohol and drugs as a coping mechanism. He was in and out of juvenile detentions and rehab facilities for teens. He bounced back and forth between my house and my ex-husband's house as frequently as a ping-pong ball. He wore his rage out in the open for everyone to see.

My son, Dan, didn't cause the trouble or demand the attention that my youngest did. But he suffered deeply, turning his pain inward. In his early teens, he went through a Goth-look stage where everything revolved around *The Rocky Horror Picture Show*. He was depressed and emotionally lost and he didn't have one responsible, mature adult in his life to turn to for direction or help. So he grew up fast and hard.

By the time he was seventeen, the black clothes were gone. He had found a job as a lighting technician trainee. He wore his hair cut short, his clothes clean-cut, and he built a life and a career that would provide for him and his future family up to this very day.

Deservedly, he also found the only way to cope was to cut his parents loose. He became emotionally distant from both of us and eventually moved out of my home to live on his own when he was still a teen.

How ironic that the child I fought so hard to keep, the child I loved more than he will ever know, the child who helped me survive a time in my life that otherwise may have destroyed me, would spend his teenage years *without* the mother he deserved— the mother I had so wanted to be.

The deep, emotional wounds I continued to harbor from the loss of my first-born son, coupled with the depression resulting from my sister's betrayal and my divorce, on top of then having to deal with my return to my mother's house, were just too much for me to handle and I emotionally shut down. It took me almost a year to get back on my feet. Almost a year to do more than sleepwalk through my life. Almost a year to become the mother I had used to be.

But it was too late for my children.

The youngest was living with his father and still wreaking havoc and pain on himself and everyone in his circle. My middle son . . .

He was brave enough to look me in the eye about a year after my divorce and say, "You can't just wake up one day and decide you're ready to be my mother again. Where were you when I needed you? Well, I don't need you now."

To this day, unfortunately, I believe he still feels that way.

He has allowed me back into his life, spends holidays and the grandchildren's birthdays with me. He encourages my relationship with his children and I strive to be the best grandmother I can be.

I know somewhere deep inside he loves me. Of that I have no doubt. But I'm afraid the damage went too deep and lasted too long for us to ever be able to repair our relationship back to the wonderful, loving, close relationship we had when he was a child. The relationship that I remember and he has long forgotten.

My son has not learned how to forgive.

I don't blame him for that in any way.

He has had no one to teach him compassion or forgiveness, to comfort him during life's deepest trials. That, I have learned, only God can do.

I don't think my son understands that forgiveness does not absolve me from any of the things I did or any of the pain I caused. Forgiveness is for *him*. So he can find a way to release the pent up hurt and anger, to get rid of the bitterness I know continues to live within him. I pray every day of my life that he finds his path to forgiveness . . . not for me, I will never deserve it.

When my son, Dan, met his brother, Steve, for the first time, he gave him a light man-hug in which they tapped one another's arms and it lasted all of three seconds. Later, though, after the two of them had had some time to talk and get to know one another a little bit, Dan said to Steve, "You're the lucky one. You met our mother at a good time and a good place in her life. You weren't raised by her."

How horribly heartbreaking it is for me to acknowledge that those words were true.

Chapter

6

Steve

When I was growing up, there wasn't a fast food building on every corner. You didn't have the McDonald's, Wendy's, Burger King, and others that you have today. Most blue-collar workers brown-bagged it for lunch.

In those days, Sam's Club or Costco didn't yet exist. The local grocery stores didn't provide party trays.

My father drove a lunch truck. He'd service construction sites and businesses, filling the lunch orders of the local workers. He made a quality product, providing good home-cooked food at a good price. His business thrived and grew. Before long, he owned several lunch trucks.

His reputation for good food grew and he found himself selling his food to other lunch-truck drivers, too. Before long, he had built his business to the point where he was ready to take the next step and open his own deli/catering business.

I was proud of my father. He'd built this business with a lot of hard work. He put in long hours, often starting his day at four a.m. and not ending until well past the rest of the world's quitting time. He devoted himself to providing a quality product at an affordable price.

I was about seventeen when I started working for my dad. He paid me well. More than any of my other friends ever got. I bought my own car. I always had money in my pocket. Being a typical kid, I didn't appreciate the large paycheck I earned unless I was flashing around what that money bought.

I never wanted for anything—except maybe freedom.

While my friends were playing ball or hanging out, I was rolling meat for party trays or slicing celery and onions for salads. I worked after school and, as my father's business grew, most weekends. I began to hate the sight of salads and meats. I began to resent always having to work when it appeared to me the rest of the kids my age were out having fun.

At times, I was frustrated. When my dad and I argued or when I missed an outing with some of the guys that I hadn't wanted to miss, the recollection that I was adopted snuck into my mind.

On at least one occasion, I would actually think "You're not my father!" during a heated debate.

Of course, in hindsight, I wish I'd never had those thoughts. My father was a good man and didn't deserve those words from me.

But I *was* adopted.

I wasn't his biological child.

And no matter how much I loved him or he loved me, the truth of that situation was beginning to impact our lives.

As a teenager, I didn't give much thought to my birth mother. I didn't lie awake at night and wonder what she looked like or who she was. She really wasn't important to me at all one way or the other.

My adoptive parents had provided me with a great childhood. I never felt rejected or unloved. I spent most of my life never thinking about the situation at all. My birth mother was nothing more to me than a mild curiosity. Except for those unexpected, unpredictable moments when she would creep into my mind.

I never knew what triggered those thoughts. They'd just show up and take residence in my mind. I'd be driving my car. Maybe I'd be just walking down the street. Maybe I'd just had a particularly hard day at work. Nothing in particular that I can remember would trigger these thoughts but they'd come anyway. I'd hear that little voice in the back of my head. The voice that would remind me I had a parallel life out there. It grew louder over time.

Of course, as a teenager I always fantasized that the other life was better. You know, bigger, more exciting, whatever. The grass-is-always-greener syndrome I guess. I'd fantasize that maybe my mother had married my father and I had brothers and sisters out there. Or if not my father, I was pretty sure she had probably gone on to marry and have more children so I'd have half-brothers and half-sisters. For an only child, I have to admit it was an intriguing and interesting fantasy.

Maybe my mother was rich and lived in a big fancy house and drove a cool car.

Material things didn't matter to me. Honestly, they didn't.

But on days when I'd have to work in my father's catering business, rolling meat for party trays instead of being able to go out with my friends, the thought of a rich, catering-free life had quite an appeal to a teenager.

The voice inside my head didn't crop up very often. But when it did, it planted seeds and those seeds started to grow.

Most of the emotions I dealt with at that time weren't overwhelming. I didn't stay awake at night worrying about any of it. The word *pretend* kept coming to mind, though. It's a shame, really. I don't want to belittle my relationship with my parents in any way because I love them. But I seem to be a very analytical, down-to-earth, call-things-as-they-are type person. It's just the way I'm wired and this word *pretend* just wouldn't go away.

I know that word may seem harsh for some people to hear but, in its simplest form, that was my truth. We were all pretending. My adoptive parents were pretending they were my parents. I was pretending I was their son. My grandparents were pretending they were my grandparents.

It didn't mean that we didn't love one another. I loved my parents, and still do as much as I possibly could, and my parents loved me as much as they possibly could. I know that.

But we all knew that I wasn't their flesh and blood, that I was born to someone else, that I belonged in someone else's DNA gene pool, so we pretended.

Slowly, that voice inside my head bothered me with more and more frequency. I began to wonder who I really was, where I came from and where I belonged. I also began to understand that someday it would be more than an occasional thought or a teenage musing. Someday I would need to know the answers to those questions.

Diane

It took a long time to recover from my divorce. Step one was climbing out of my depressive state long enough to care about what was happening to me and to my children. Eventually I did.

First order of business was to move out of my parent's home. That had been a particularly painful place to try and recover, anyway.

As I said in the beginning of this story, my mother didn't like most of her kids, but she loved my sister. As adults, my mother and sister had been more like best friends than mother and daughter. They saw one another daily, went shopping together, were in and out of each other's home with regularity and even belonged to the same bowling team.

When my sister moved away from Michigan to live with me in New Jersey, my mother was crushed. She couldn't understand why my sister would ever choose living with me over living with her and, truthfully, it added to her hatred of me. When the divorce hit, my family rallied around me in support. My mother . . . not so much.

One particular morning about five months after my separation, I was walking down the stairs and I could hear my mother sobbing at the base of them. When she saw me, she raced up the steps, meeting me on the stairwell. She was screaming at me and totally out of control.

I really don't know what had set her off, only that she was actually grieving the loss of my sister who had been her one true friend. Something must have happened or been said that morning to trigger my mother's emotions.

"You never should have moved her into your house!" she yelled. "This is all your fault! If you had been a decent wife to your husband, he wouldn't have gone looking for someone else. Now look what you've done!"

I honestly can't remember what I said back to her. I'm sure it was mean and loud and cruel. All I know is that the situation on that landing turned ugly. She grabbed my hair and slammed my head into the wall.

"You are not the Virgin Mary!" she screamed. "And your sister isn't the scarlet woman. You did this! You did this and I'm sick of everyone cutting your sister out of our lives! Why did you take her in with you? Why?"

She went downstairs, grabbed her jacket, and stormed out the door for one of her long walks down Blood Road.

My father had been sitting at the kitchen table. Although he hadn't witnessed the encounter, he had certainly heard it. I stormed into the kitchen.

"You heard that!" I accused.

He nodded but didn't look up from the paper.

"I can't take it anymore. She's blaming me for all of this!"

"What can I do?" he asked, laying the paper on the table. "How can I help? I'll do anything to help."

"Get me out of this house," I said.

And he did.

———

Within the week, my father helped move me into a cute little rental home about an hour south of Oakland. We were finally and forever out of my mother's home. My children, ages nine and eleven, and I were starting a new chapter in our lives and I tried hard not to choke on the fear of doing it alone.

I found a job as a secretary in a law firm. That didn't last long. Not because I didn't like the job but because it paid only a couple of dollars over minimum wage. I was struggling financially and didn't know how I was going to continue paying for this home much longer on my own.

My ex-husband sent $40 a week child support, which was supposed to cover all the needs of two children. Our assets had been split down the middle, including the bills, and after I paid for my lawyer and paid my mother more than $1,200 for support for the months I had lived with her, there wasn't much left of my settlement. Money was getting really tight and I was scared.

I knew I had to find another job. I had to earn a man's wage if I was going to support a family. But how? I didn't have a college education and I definitely didn't have a trade like plumber or mechanic.

One night I saw an ad in the classified section of the newspaper: SELL FUN! FUN! FUN! IF YOU ARE A PEOPLE PERSON, IF YOU ENJOY SHOWING FAMILIES HOW THEY CAN BUILD A LIFETIME OF HAPPY MEMORIES, CALL US TODAY FOR AN INTERVIEW.

Sell fun? I could do that. And I was all for families and happy memories. I called the number and went in for an interview.

It turns out the position was for a timeshare salesperson. I had never even heard of timeshare, didn't have a clue what it was. All I did know was that a bell kept ringing, people kept cheering, and those sales people were making money, more money than any secretary I ever knew. I wanted the job.

The manager of the business, a kind, sweet, lovely Indian man named Paul found out in the interview that I was a single mother with two young boys and he all but threw me out of his office.

"Go home, missus. This is not the job for you. You have two children who depend on you. Go home."

I didn't understand he was sincerely trying to help me out. He knew that the timeshare business was sporadic and unpredictable. You could make some very good commissions, but those commission checks could be few and very far between.

I was desperate. Every single night for a week, I showed up at the office and begged for a chance.

Paul kept sending me home. I kept coming back.

About five days into this back and forth dance that Paul and I were caught up in, one of the salesmen, Freddie, approached Paul on my behalf.

"Why don't you give her a chance?" he asked. "What do you have to lose? It's all commission, anyway. Seems to me if she has the bulldog tenacity to keep showing up here she just might turn out to be pretty good. Besides, if she can't hack it, she'll be gone in no time anyway."

Paul looked from Freddie to me and then gave in. "Okay," he said. He handed me a book filled with pictures of beautiful resorts throughout the United States. "Go sit behind that man. Don't say anything. Don't do anything. Just look at this book and listen."

I instantly did what he said before he could change his mind. The salesman's presentation took about an hour and a half. It included a ten minute movie of a resort in Florida called the Outrigger Beach Club followed by the dollars and cents of what it would cost to belong.

My vacations had always been sleeping at family residences and going to the beach. This book held thousands of beautiful places with everything you could ever want to see or do. Mountains. Beaches. White-water rafting. Horseback riding. Gambling in Vegas. I didn't just want to sell the product, I wanted to sign on the dotted line and have this life for myself and my kids, too.

After I listened to the entire presentation, I ran into Paul's office.

"Please," I said, "You have to let me do this."

"Okay. You've got the book. I'll give you a couple. Go for it. After you show them the movie, call Bob over to close the deal for you."

"What? What about training? Isn't there training?" I asked.

"You had your training. You wanted a chance. I'm giving you one. Now, go introduce yourself to the next couple waiting in the lobby."

My heart beat so fast, I thought it was going to explode. But I was also happy and excited and hopeful that my life was about to change for the better. Perhaps it was my enthusiasm or my honesty of what I thought about the product at the time because I certainly had no formal sales experience, but my first couple bought. They bought two red weeks, which was prime time in the Florida resort, and they paid full price.

I'd never been told that nobody pays full price. That's why closers like Bob are called in. They are management. They are authorized to sell "back in inventory" properties. People are already sold on the idea of owning timeshare so when the price drops by thousands, many of them sign on the dotted line, believing they are getting an incredible deal.

I didn't have to call Bob to my table. My couple bought right after the movie. I will never forget the look of astonishment on Paul, Freddie, and Bob's faces when I walked over and asked them if someone could help me fill out the paperwork.

My first commission check was more money than I had made in four weeks as a secretary. It was also the last commission check I got for almost two months. No matter how hard I tried or what I'd do after that night, one couple after another turned me down. But I refused to give up. I had done it once. I could do it again.

One day I was sitting in the break room when an older gentleman, a quiet salesman who didn't mingle with the rest of us and usually kept to himself, approached me and asked if he could sit at my table for a moment.

I nodded.

"You seem to be having a run of bad luck," he said.

I nodded again.

"Would you like me to help you? If you'll give me some of your time, I'll show you how I sell this product."

I knew this man wasn't the top salesperson on the floor but he wasn't the worst either. He sold regularly enough to make me feel he just might have something to offer.

"Sure," I said. "I'd be grateful for any help I can get."

He sat down. "My name's Bill."

"Hi, Bill. I'm Diane."

He smiled at me. "Let's get started."

Bill quickly became my mentor, my best friend, and eventually my second husband. He was twenty-one years older than me and had never been married. He had poor health, was overweight, and was a shy little man with a curmudgeon side to him that rubbed many people the wrong way.

But he was a good man, a moral man, and he fell head over heels in love with me. I wish I could have loved him back. I really, really do, because he certainly deserved it.

When he asked me to marry him, I accepted for all the wrong reasons. He was good to me and to my kids. The three of us were a package deal and Bill would take all of us on dates to movies or dinner or whatever. He didn't make a lot of money, but he was willing to throw what he did make into the joint pot, which made my financial life much easier. Most of all, he was my best friend. I trusted him. I confided in him. I truly enjoyed spending time with him—and I was tired of being alone—so I accepted.

The boys accepted Bill at first. They didn't like him, but they didn't dislike him either—until we announced our wedding. If I married Bill, then any hope they had of their father and I getting back together would be gone. They resented Bill from that day on and acted out on many, many occasions throughout their teenage years.

The night before the wedding, I got cold feet. Not for me—I still believed marrying Bill would benefit me in a myriad of ways—but for him. He deserved better. He deserved someone who loved him back. So the night before our wedding, I went to call it off.

He had been staying overnight at my house and the children and I had been staying overnight at my brother's—the "can't see the bride before the wedding" scenario. But now that there wasn't going to be a wedding, I went back to my house to let him know.

It was about three o'clock in the morning when I quietly let myself into the house. The light was on in the bedroom. As I approached, what I saw broke my heart. He had his suit and shirt and tie laid out on the bed. He was sitting on the edge of the bed, polishing his shoes and humming a tune under his breath. When he saw me standing in the doorway, he stopped.

"Hello, darling. What are you doing home?"

I sat down beside him.

"Bill, we have to talk."

"Okay."

I knew what I was going to do would break his heart, but I told myself it would be better to hurt him now than make him miserable later.

"Bill, I'm sorry. I really am, but I am not going to marry you."

"What?"

"I know my timing is terrible and I'm sorry. I really am. Don't show up tomorrow. I'll tell everyone the wedding is off. There's no need for you to be embarrassed."

"I don't understand. Why are you doing this?"

I took his hands in mine. "Because I don't love you, Bill, and you deserve to be loved."

He studied me for a moment and then asked, "Do you like me?"

"Of course I like you. You're my best friend."

"Well, maybe you'll grow to love me."

My eyes filled with tears. "I won't, Bill. I'm so sorry but I know I won't."

He patted my hands. "That's all right. As long as you like me, then we can make it work. You see, darling, I love you enough for both of us."

By now, tears trickled down my cheeks. "Please, Bill. Please don't make this more difficult for either one of us than it has to be. Please don't show up tomorrow. Please. I'll tell everyone that you changed your mind."

He let go of my hand, picked up his shoe, and continued polishing it.

"I'm going to be there. Hopefully, after you get a few hours sleep, you will be there, too."

He kept his word. When I arrived at the justice of the peace and was escorted into a room where my family and all my coworkers were already waiting, I saw Bill, wearing the biggest grin on his face and dressed in his Sunday finest, standing in front of the judge.

Maybe Bill was right. Maybe being best friends would be enough.

When the judge started the section of the ceremony that began with, "Will you, William, take Diane as your lawfully wedded wife . . . ," Bill never waited for the rest of it. He never listened for the "for better, for worse, for richer, for poorer, in sickness and in health" stuff.

Instead, he yelled, "I will! I will! I will! I will!"

The whole room burst into laughter, including the judge, and I knew then that it was going to be all right. I would be a loving and loyal companion to this man for the rest of his life and he would continue to be my best friend and a companion to me. We could make it work, and we did for twenty years, until he died in September 2007.

Shortly after we married in 1986, we packed up the kids and moved to Florida.

We rarely made it back to Michigan after that move. My relationship with my mother became nothing more than a couple of telephone calls a month and a gift on Mother's Day and Christmas. Slowly, over the years, my mother's memory worsened and, when I was forty, she was diagnosed with Alzheimer's. Soon the telephone calls were to my father because my mother no longer was capable of holding conversations.

Florida turned out to be a good move for us. We knew there were plenty of timeshare properties there and employment would not be a problem. We were starting a new life together and we both wanted a fresh start. What better place to do it than in the world of Disney where dreams come true.

Chapter

7

Steve

On my twenty-first birthday, I went to Atlantic City with my parents and a friend. I'm not exactly sure why I wanted to go there. Probably a bit of nostalgia. I knew I'd been born in Atlantic City.

So I sat with my parents at a bar and had my first legal drink. I went to the casino at the Claridge Hotel and gambled for the very first time. I had a great birthday.

I had started thinking more and more about my mother. Especially on my birthdays. She may have been able to forget about me the rest of the year, but she had to be thinking about me on this particular day, wouldn't she?

So birthdays became days of reflection and wondering. Was my mother still alive and out there someplace? Was she remembering this one day, this special day unique to just the two of us? Was she thinking of me? Did she ever regret giving me away? Did she ever miss me?

So I came to Atlantic City on my twenty-first birthday, the day society considered me an adult. I told my parents it was because I wanted to drink for the first time and try my hand at gambling. The truth of the matter was that I wanted to feel closer to my mother. In what better place could I do that than in the city where I had been born?

Diane

Thank God for red lights.

One day, just for fun or out of boredom, I told myself I was going to time how long the wait was at this particular light. Traffic officers could top off their monthly quota of tickets just nabbing the yellow light pedal-to-the-medal speed racers trying to avoid the wait.

I was behind the wheel of our van, waiting for the light to change, when another one of those moments in life, the kind that sneak up on you and rock you to the core, came from the most unlikely source. My husband, Bill, sat in the passenger seat. My boys, Dan and David, were in the back.

"Mom, is it true I have another brother out there some-place?" David asked.

My gaze flew to the rearview mirror and connected with my youngest son's eyes.

"Who told you that?"

I was shocked and upset and furious. No one had the right to tell him that information except me. How did he find out? Did my ex-husband tell him? Did my sister? Who would have told an eleven-year-old child he had a half-brother he didn't know, and why?

"Mom?"

I could see David in the mirror. He didn't move a muscle. He simply stared back at me, surprise and shock evident in his expression. Dan remained silent.

"Who told you? Did your father tell you?"

"Nobody told me. The thought just popped into my head so I asked."

"Don't lie to me. I want to know. Your father told you, didn't he? Why? Why would he do that?"

David's eyes glistened with tears. "Nobody told me, Mom. I swear."

"Then how did you know?"

"Is it true, Mom? Is it true?" His voice held a sense of wonder and a tear slid down his cheek.

I forced myself to calm down. Anger wasn't going to get the answers I needed and it was obvious my anger was upsetting him. I took several deep breaths and, when I spoke again, I forced myself to remain calm.

"David, I'm sorry I yelled. You surprised me, that's all." I turned my head and looked at him through the opening between the front bucket seats. "I promise I won't yell anymore."

David looked me straight in the eye. "Nobody told me, Mom. Honest. I just knew."

"How, David? Nobody just thinks up something like that."

He shrugged his shoulders. "I did. I swear, Mom. It's the truth."

Seconds of silence passed between us like an eternity.

He seemed so sincere, so genuine. Was it possible he was telling the truth? I know that it had been *years* since I had had any conversation with anyone about my missing son. It definitely wasn't something he would have ever been able to overhear in my house.

And it didn't make any sense that he would have heard it in Danny's house.

Danny and I weren't on good terms—it had been a bitter and a nasty divorce—but he'd have no reason to try and hurt me this way. Even if he had, I knew without doubt that he wouldn't use his son to do it.

I had heard stories about twins separated at birth who still had some kind of intuitive ties to the other sibling. Granted, David and my first-born son weren't twins, although they did both carry the same name and some of the same DNA. Could it be possible? Is there a spiritual tie between us that sometimes we're not even aware exists? Is there some kind of invisible bond in families?

I didn't understand what was happening in the van that day—and I still don't today. I can only relate events the way they happened.

"Mom? Is it true?"

I looked into David's eyes and saw hurt and confusion and maybe even a little bit of fear.

"We'll talk about it when we get home."

The light finally turned green.

Once home, I sat my sons down and I told them about their brother and the adoption. I told them I hadn't wanted to give their brother away, that I wanted very much to keep him and that I missed him every day of my life. But I also told them that it had been the best thing for the baby, that I wasn't in a position at that time in my life to be a good mom or give the baby a good life. I told David I had received a letter from the adoption agency telling me that the baby's father was an engineer and his mother was a school teacher. That they had tried for more than five years to have a child of their own and couldn't, so they were very happy to have David Brett come live with them.

"Is that his name, Mom? David Brett? Did you name me after him?" David's stare was intense.

"I named him David Brett because it means 'dearly beloved.' I don't know if his adoptive parents kept the name. But I hoped if they did, or at least let him know that that was his name on his original birth certificate, that he would discover what it meant and he would know that he'd been loved."

I stroked my son's head.

"Yes, honey, I did name you David. Just like people name their children after favorite uncles who passed away or grand-parents that are gone. You help me always have a memory, a little piece of that baby with me. But I named *you* David Mark, not Brett, so you would always be your own person with your own name and your own identity."

That seemed to satisfy him. The subject of adoption or lost brothers never came up in our household again. But I found out years later that, like all secrets, just because it wasn't spoken aloud didn't mean it had gone away. The sub-ject was very much alive in our minds, our lives, and our hearts. When Dave did meet his brother, Steve, for the very first time, I'd find out just how much he'd thought of him as the years passed.

That conversation soon led to another one just as painful and just as difficult. I called my mother.

"Hi, Mom."

"Hi. How are you? How are the boys?"

"Fine. Everyone's fine."

We spoke for about five minutes, exchanging pleasantries and catching up on the daily activities worth mentioning, as well as the weather and anything else that came to mind. It was like every other conversation we ever had—superficial, shallow, meaningless.

"Mom, David asked me a question the other day. He asked me about his half-brother."

The silence on the line was so thick, it reminded me of high humidity on a summer day, invisible but there, so uncomfort-able everyone wished it would just go away.

"How did he find out?" The anger in her voice, the unspoken censure that I must have been the one to tell him, came across the line as if she had spoken those thoughts aloud.

"I don't know who told him."

"What do you mean you don't know who told him?"

"Look, it isn't important right now how he found out. What's important is that he knows."

"You could have told him it wasn't true."

"It *is* true."

Again the silence. Heavy. Oppressive. Almost painful.

"I sat both the boys down and explained everything," I said, my voice filling the uncomfortable silence between us.

Then came the storm.

"What's the matter with you? Won't you ever learn? Why would you tell them something like that? We went to all the trouble and expense to make this all go away. We gave you a clean slate to start your life over. But you just can't let it go, can you? You had to make sure you told your brothers and sisters. Now you've gone and told your sons! Everything we did, we did for you, and you just keep throwing it away."

"They have a right to know."

"They don't have a right to know!" she screamed at the top of her lungs. "It's over! It's been over for years. Damn it, Diane, why can't you leave it alone?"

Tears rolled down my cheeks.

"Because I can't, Mom. I can't. I lost my baby . . . and it hurts . . . and it never stops hurting . . . and I can't find a way to let it go."

Silence.

This time not angry and oppressive. This time defeated.

"Then find him. You've undone everything your father and I ever did for you, anyway. We tried to give you a second chance. We've kept your secret. You've gone and told the world. So if you miss him so damn much, then why don't you go and find him?" She sounded weary and exasperated and maybe even a little hurt.

"I can't."

"Why not?"

"For two reasons. You burned the adoption papers. I don't even know the name of the agency we used. I don't have a clue how to even start looking."

Silence.

"Besides, he isn't my son anymore." I heard the truth in my words and the pain was almost unbearable. "He has parents who love him, who are devoting their lives to raising him. I don't have any right to show up on their doorstep unannounced and threaten the world they've built."

Seconds of silence stretched like eons between us.

"Every once in a while you have a moment of maturity and sanity," my mother said when she finally spoke. "I wish to God you would use it more often."

"You don't have to worry. I have no intention of ever hurting those parents. No matter what you think of me, I could never do that." My voice took on a longing that even I didn't recognize at the time. "But I'm telling you right now, Mom, if he ever looks for me . . . if he ever wants to know who I am . . . my door will be wide open."

She hung up the phone without saying another word.

Steve

Throughout the years, I continued to keep most of my thoughts about being adopted at bay.

I fell in love and married a woman who was then, and is still today, my soul mate. No one has ever connected with me on every level of life as deeply or profoundly as Barbara. I don't know how I ever was lucky enough for her to give me the time of day, but she did. We've been married for twenty years and I can't imagine my life without her.

She was divorced with three children when we married. I became an instant step-father and took on the role seriously and happily. It was during these early years when the conversation turned to my birth mother.

My wife would tell me about her family history, particularly focusing on health issues. She had grandparents who had lived into their nineties and one had lived to one hundred.

I couldn't be as forthcoming.

I didn't have a clue who I was. I had no history. I had no idea what diseases, like diabetes or heart disease or cancer, ran in my biological family. I had no idea what signs to watch for or what annual screenings to have done. It hadn't ever bothered me before, but now that I was married and we were contemplating having a family of our own, the fact that I was adopted took on a totally new importance.

It didn't sit well with me or my wife that I might not be able to protect my family because I didn't have the common information that most other families had at their fingertips. My wife suggested I might want to look into searching for my biological mother if for no other reason than for health information. I listened to her suggestion and I even thought about it for a little bit.

But life was good.

I was happily married to my best friend, raising three wonderful kids, and both of us were working our butts off trying to provide our family with the American dream. A biological mother who had given me away more than two decades ago was not a priority to me. Not yet.

Who would have ever thought
I'd get all my answers by
phone in 2012?

My parents

This is me at the American Christian Fiction Writers conference where I was a finalist for the prestigious Carol Award.

Steve as a baby, about three months old

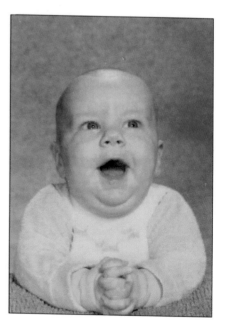

Steve at Christmas.

Steve on a motorcycle.

Steve waiting for a flying lesson to begin.

This was the first time Steve met any of his family besides Dave and me. Top row: Barb, Steve, Me, Sandy (Mike's wife), Mike, their daughter Megan. Bottom row: Claudia, Dan, my brother Tom who passed away June 2013, and his wife, Benie.

Me, Steve, and his adoptive mother, Nancy. When Steve introduced us to family and friends he said, "This is the mother who made me and this is the mother who made me who I am today."

Steve and Barb at their favorite vacation spot, Sanibel Island, Florida.

Steve and Barb

My son Dan, me, and Steve

Steve, me, and my youngest son David

My daughter-in-law, Esther, and me at Steve's house for my grandson's graduation.

Steve and me at his mother-in-law's birthday party, in Sanibel Island, 2012.

When I held my first-born son, Steven, in my arms, I felt a wave of emotion. This was my flesh and blood, my biological son and neither one of us would ever have to pretend otherwise. I thought of my biological mother. I wondered how she had felt when she'd held me for the first time or even if she had held me at all. I wondered what circumstances could have made her carry me for nine months through all the discomforts of pregnancy, endure the pain of labor and delivery, only to turn around and give me away.

For the first time in my life, I thought about my mother as a real, live human being and not a fantasy in my mind. I'd just watched what my wife had endured giving birth to our son. How could any mother go through what my wife had and then go home with empty arms? I was surprised at the emotion rising up in me. I felt sorry for my mother. I did. She was the one who had experienced a loss, not me.

I was fine.

I'd had a good life.

I didn't feel I needed my birth mother in my life. I already had a mother. I didn't have any conscious desire at that point to find her. Not yet, anyway. Those thoughts and plans would still be years away.

But for the briefest instant when I looked down into my son's face, the first niggling thoughts crossed my mind about what it might entail to actually start a search. I wondered if I *could* find her, and I wondered how it might change my life if I did.

Chapter

8

Diane

In the years following my divorce from Danny, my life slowly took shape.

I remarried, again not a love match, but this time a warm, affectionate companionship with a much older gentleman who cared about me and my children. He wasn't financially success-ful in his life. He worked at various sales jobs selling solar pan-els or timeshare and made barely enough to get by.

Once Bill retired, he was able to draw a very small social security check that barely covered his medications, placing the responsibility of earning a living on my shoulders. But that was okay. I didn't marry him for his money. I married him because he was my best friend. He understood me better than anyone else ever did. And he loved me, unconditionally.

That was a novelty for me. I truly hadn't had very many people in my life ever make me feel loved or special. During our marriage, I managed to put myself through college. It took me five years instead of four since I had to work during the day for the first three years to help support us, but eventually I earned my degree in occupational therapy, which allowed me to build a lucrative career.

I also took an interest in writing. I joined Romance Writers of America and became active in the local Volusia County Romance Writers chapter in Florida. I made friends there who have been with me through good times and bad. I am proud to say they are still my friends today.

Bill loved the idea that he was married to a potential author. He'd read all my work. He'd travel with me to the annual romance conventions. He'd brag to everyone and anyone about his wife, the writer. Bill believed in me long before I believed in myself. It has always been my one great regret of our relationship that he didn't live long enough to see that dream come true. He was my staunchest supporter.

But with God, all things are possible, so who knows? I'd like to believe that somehow Bill was there when I got the call from the New York office that Harlequin wanted to publish my first novel. Maybe he even put in a good word for me upstairs and helped it happen.

During our marriage, minus a few years when we lived in Tennessee to take care of Bill's mom before she died, we made Florida our home. My sons were grown and gone in 1998 when Bill and I moved into a senior mobile home community. We lived there until Bill died in 2007 from pancreatic cancer. I lost my best friend, my sole companion, and my hope.

Again, I plummeted into depression, this time my deepest one to date. This time I didn't just wish I was dead, but I actually made a plan and put things in motion to assure I would be.

But God intervened.

In July 2007, I had started going to church at the request of my husband and my youngest son. Dave, by this time, was a recovered alcoholic/drug addict who was a born-again Christian and devoted to the Lord. He kept in touch with me frequently.

He was strongly pushing me to discover the world's best kept secret for happiness and success—a personal and real relationship with God. Dave had picked up the pieces of his life. He was living in a new state and dating a wonderful Christian woman who knew everything about his past but loved him anyway.

Dan and his family lived a little more than an hour away. They had spent Christmas with me just the day before. But I knew it would be months, probably Easter, before he would visit me again.

The days and the nights of my life were empty and unbearably lonely. I suppose when a person hates themselves then the worst thing you can possibly do to them is put them in solitary confinement where the only human being you see or speak to day after day is yourself.

My new church family knew I was grieving over the loss of my husband. They sent cards. Some of the members dropped by now and then for unannounced visits just to say hi and see if I needed anything. But on the whole, hours would stretch into days, days into weeks, weeks into months, and the reality that I would be facing the rest of my life alone began to set deep into my bones.

I don't handle alone well.

I had been the oldest of seven children. The youngest ones had always been my shadow. I left that home for one of my own and spent almost two decades raising children. I also cared for two mother-in-laws at various times in my life until they passed. In 1999 my sister and I moved my parents to Florida. We helped care for my mother until her death in 2003 and my father's death in 2005. My sister moved out of state after my father's death. Bill was the only person I had left in my life on a daily basis and now, in 2007, he was gone, too.

I remember after my divorce from Danny and my remarriage to Bill, and long after I'd worked to put myself through college, having a conversation with my mother. In the course of that conversation, she'd told me that she'd always thought that I was a strong person, that I was a survivor, one of the few compliments she had bestowed on me in our years together. She was right. I had survived a multitude of tough breaks and bad choices. But being alone, I wasn't strong anymore.

My depression had no end in sight.

Three months had passed since Bill's death and it was the Christmas season. The day I decided to take my life I had made plans. I was going to put my dogs in a kennel. I was going to pack a bag, drive to the beach at dusk when the beach would be empty and the lifeguard gone, lay things out on the deserted sand so it would look like an accident, and then swim into the ocean. I love the ocean and couldn't think of a better way to die. I intended to swim as far and for as long as I possibly could so that even if I panicked and changed my mind, I wouldn't have the strength or the energy to swim back.

I sat down at my computer to type my youngest son, David, a letter. I knew my death would be the most difficult for him. He was so invested in healing our relationship, in seeing that I found my way to God. I wanted to make sure he understood there was nothing he could have done to stop me. I strongly felt I needed to explain to him how much I was suffering and how desperately I needed to stop this pain. I'd lived with pain, disappointment, betrayal, and loss my entire life and had been strong enough to survive. But now I was facing the daunting task of living with myself and I hated myself too much to do that.

Depressed, suicidal people are selfish. They don't think of anyone at the time but themselves. They can't see further than their pain and they don't have the energy to search for an alternative solution to their situation or sometimes even the energy to ask for help. They just want the pain to end and they don't care how it does. I was one of those people.

When I sat down at my computer, I checked my email. It's something I do automatically and I didn't give it any conscious thought. Until I saw the long list of emails waiting for me.

I didn't recognize any of the email addresses but I was intrigued and opened them. What happened next took my breath away.

The emails had come from people all over the country. I specifically remember places like North Carolina, Texas, and even one from Washington state, places I had never been. Not one name was familiar. I had never met even one of these people and to this day I still haven't.

But they saved my life.

They were all writers who had heard about the loss of my husband back in September on the various loops online that we all frequent and now that the holidays were here and they knew I was facing my first holiday season as a widow, I must have been on their mind.

And each and every email had a common thread. They read:

"God spoke to my heart and told me to contact you in this hour of pain . . ."

"It came upon my heart to contact you and let you know in this difficult time that you are not alone."

"Holiday seasons are always the worst. My prayers are with you on this first Christmas without your husband. I will keep you in my prayers."

"You are not alone. When you feel beaten and so down that there is no where to go, look up."

And the emails continued. More than a dozen of them. Encouraging me. Uplifting me. Reminding me that I was not alone and that God was beside me every step of the way through this dark and difficult time in my life.

It worked.

I distinctly remember sitting at my computer, tears flowing down my face, sighing heavily and speaking out loud.

"Okay, God. We'll try it your way. I can't handle my life anymore. This ship is sinking. So I'm going to move over and let you take the wheel. Help me, Lord. Please, please help me."

I'm not going to lie and say that everything instantly improved or that I never shed another tear or that I never had another depressing day.

But every day after that one was better than the one before.

Steve

In 2005, I moved my family from New Jersey to the South in pursuit of a lucrative job opportunity. It was a major decision and one I would regret multiple times over the years, despite it working out well for all of us.

I moved my wife away from her large and close-knit extended family. I moved my children away from their older brother and sister, their cousins, their aunts and uncles, their maternal grandparents, their friends, and their school.

I'm grateful for the job. It has provided me with a good living that, in turn, has allowed me to live in a bigger house and provide a better quality of life for my family than I ever would have been able to afford if I had remained in New Jersey. It is providing me with a lucrative pension so my wife, Barb, and I can have a financially safe and comfortable retirement. None of it came without cost. But isn't that what life is? Compromise? It all comes down to give and take and how much of each you can live with.

My adoptive parents sold their business, moved to the same state, and bought a house a short commute from our home. My wife flew back to New Jersey several times a year to visit her family and, occasionally, they came to us. My children adjusted to their new schools, their new lives, and made new friends.

Everything should have been ideal.

But it wasn't.

I never could shake the feeling that I had made a major mistake in moving away from New Jersey. I grew depressed and moody and complained on many occasions that I thought we should pack up and move back.

Barbara, besides being my wife, the mother of my children, and the love of my life, is also my anchor. She understands me better than any other human being on Earth and loves me deeply despite my flaws and short-comings. She is the voice of reason when I tune out the world and am not thinking reasonably myself.

Every time I complained about the move, she'd put on her anchor cap. She'd point out to me that no matter how much we might like to return to New Jersey, it wouldn't be a realistic move. We could never provide the same lifestyle back there that we were giving our children here. She also, being more spiritual than me, would point out that everything in life happens for a reason.

"Steve," she said. "I don't know why we're here. We may never know or understand why we're here. But I believe that God put us here for a reason and in the end it will all work out for the good."

Little did I know at the time that just a couple of years later I would discover just how right my wife had been. If I had remained in New Jersey and never moved, then my relationship with my original mother when I met her would have been markedly different. We would have seen one another once or twice a year at best instead of the frequency we see each other now simply because of finances and distance. Yeah, everything happens for a reason. I just didn't know it at the time.

In the meantime, I lived my life. I went to work, took care of the house, raised my kids, spent time with my family. But I wasn't completely happy. I had an emptiness inside that I kept thinking was connected to the New Jersey move. I let it affect my mood. It got so bad that my wife and kids began buying me t-shirts with a variety of sayings but the gist of it all was that the wearer was a grumpy person.

I wish it wasn't true about me but, looking back, I have to admit it was. My family put up with a lot from me for a very long time. For years, I blamed my unhappiness on working in the catering business, a business I hated and felt trapped in. Then I blamed the move to another state. I took my family from the only place I'd ever called home and the only people I'd ever known as family and I saw that as the culprit.

As true as these excuses might be, I never acknowledged that it was possible there might be an additional cause. I never admitted aloud to anyone, and truthfully not even to myself, that there was something missing deep inside me. A sense of identity. A sense of belonging. A knowledge of who I was and where I belonged in this world. That missing piece hurt. It hurt like a wound that wouldn't heal and there wasn't a thing I could do about it.

So, yeah, I guess I deserved the grumpy shirts.

A few years after our move, I think it was about 2008 or 2009, I'm not sure which, I was sitting in the living room with my family watching television when a new show came on. It was called *The Locator*. The show didn't last very long on the airwaves but even in its short lifespan it had made an indelible impact on me.

The show was hosted by a man whose mother had been adopted. He set out to help her find her biological family and did. Then, he decided to host a show and try to do the same thing for other families.

One night I was watching one of the episodes about an adoptee that was being reunited for the first time with his biological family. As I watched, I saw a room full of blood relatives gather together to meet and greet him.

Of course, I knew the situation was staged for television and geared to create the highest emotional response for the ratings. Logically, I understood how things like that work.

But when the adoptee walked into the room, when he saw his biological family for the first time, when he was greeted and hugged and welcomed by a room full of strangers, but strangers that belonged to him, his blood, his relatives, his clan—it was like I had been hit by a brick. Watching that episode was the first time that any real raw emotion I had been keeping inside, either voluntarily or involuntarily, came out.

Tears burned my eyes. Emotions I had never even realized existed inside of me sprang to the surface with such force I couldn't believe it. I didn't understand the power and force of these emotions, just that this show had somehow shaken me to my core. Not wanting to embarrass myself in front of my children by crying, I got up and walked into the kitchen.

My wife quickly followed.

I couldn't really understand at that moment why I was feeling the way I did.

My wife put her hand on my shoulder.

I looked at her and saw tears in her eyes, too.

"It's time, Steve." She smiled at me. "You need to find your mother."

Chapter

9

Diane

Life changed forever for me those final days of 2007.

I began attending Crossroads Calvary Chapel on a regular basis and learned and grew in my faith from the inspirational bible teachings of Pastor David Sharp.

My son, David, became a loving pest as he pushed and pressured me to get back into my writing and to begin attending my romance chapter meetings again.

My son, Dan, married and the father of three wonderful boys, helped open a tech business with a friend and was doing well. They actually did some events like *The Oprah Show* and once did the tech work at Radio City Music Hall.

In 2008, I entered the Daphne du Maurier Award for Excellence in Mystery and Suspense contest for unpublished authors. I was one of five finalists. My son, David, encouraged me to go to the RWA conference where the award would be announced. It was being held in San Francisco. I had never traveled alone before. I was nervous and, at first, reluctant. But with a gentle push from both my son and my writing peers in the Volusia chapter, I boarded a plane and headed for San Francisco.

I had a wonderful time. I quickly discovered that there are no strangers at a RWA conference, only romance writers who are open to quickly becoming friends. I met my future critique partner and friend, Kit Wilkinson, there. I met two women from Canada who I still correspond with today. I never had to sit at an empty table and I never ate a meal alone.

I rode a trolley car for the first time in my life. I took a boat ride out to Alcatraz prison and I sailed under the Golden Gate Bridge.

Oh yes, and I took first place in the short inspirational category romance division of the Daphne du Maurier contest.

Steve

In 2008, I began to seriously think about searching for my mother. I told myself it was for health reasons. I knew my wife still wanted the information she had asked me for when we had first married so she could be proactive in ensuring our sons' health.

I told myself that that was reason enough to search.

But deep down inside, I knew the truth.

I needed answers. Who was I? Where did I come from? Did I have other family members out there? Why was I given away? Had my mother ever wanted me? Would she want to know me now?

A popular website on the internet is ancestry.com. Many people have used their services and traced back their family histories. Some people I know were able to go all the way back to the 1500s and discover a branch of their family tree were pirates.

Fun. Entertaining. Informative.

But for me, vitally important. Something as simple as this was a monumental task I would never be able to do. I couldn't even begin because I didn't know the simplest information, like my real name.

I knew I would never be satisfied until I had the answer to the biggest question anybody has—who am I?

So I searched.

At first, I looked up the show *The Locator*. They ask tons of questions and want a significant amount of information before they agree to take on your case. Of course, I could understand their thinking. They were a television show, not a detective agency. They didn't have the time or resources to do a full-blown search and only took on the cases where their success rate in finding the people would be high.

I couldn't even tell them my birth name. I wouldn't be an easy search. I had hit my first of many dead ends.

Next, I used the Internet to search for a good private detective. It didn't take long for me to discover that most private detectives wanted much more money than I could afford to pay. Also, because I had such limited information, the search would be long, very expensive, and most likely unsuccessful.

Over the years, my adoptive parents gave me the little bit of information they had from the adoption agency in case I ever wanted to search. I knew if I decided to search that it would be in no way a negative reflection on them. I loved them. They were my parents. But I needed answers to help me understand who I really was.

What information my parents had given me was unfortunately very little. I knew my date of birth, the city I was born in, and the name of the agency that had arranged the adoption. Suddenly searching for my mother looked more like mission impossible than an achievable goal.

Since the only thing I had was the name of the adoption agency, I decided to start there. I looked up their website and read everything I could find. In small print in a drop down menu on the bottom of their page, a heading caught my eye. It read: ADOPTEES TRYING TO FIND BIRTH PARENTS. I clicked on it and actually read through a whole series of papers. I discovered that they did, indeed, try and search for your parents if you wanted to look for them.

So I filled out the application and submitted it.

A few days, maybe a week later, I received a phone call. Since I no longer lived in New Jersey and I couldn't go in and talk with the social worker in person, I was asked if I would take part in an interview over the phone. It took about a half hour or so.

The biggest question the social worker, Pat, had for me was if I was prepared to handle whatever the search turned up. She told me that not every situation turned out to be a suburban house with a white picket fence and a dog in the yard and people just dancing around waiting to meet you.

She described multiple negative scenarios. Often drugs could be involved and it was possible that my parents could turn out to be criminals. Maybe they'd turn out to be hostile, not happy about my reappearance in their lives and I'd be facing a world of hurt and rejection. Many times there are negative family situations that may have led to it. She stressed that there are a million reasons why I may have been given up for adoption and that, unfortunately, the odds were pretty good that I might not like what I find.

Pat also reminded me it was possible my mother never told anybody about me or the adoption, including her husband if she had gone on with her life and married. I had to admit that that was one of my biggest fears. What if nobody was told and I came back into the picture? The last thing I wanted to do was break up a marriage or damage a family.

Those were the things that really concerned me. I would have rather not had any information and never found my mother if I knew that all I was going to do was cause a total collapse of her family structure or negatively disrupt her life. That was never my intention.

In hindsight, I now know that whenever you do make contact with the other person, it doesn't matter what your intentions were—negativity or change, at the very least, is going to happen. If the search is successful, you're going to open up the floodgates of years gone by for that other person. In my case, flash forward to today, I could have never known then that it would have opened up so many wounds for my mother.

Those are the things I feel responsible for because I'm the one who did the searching—those are the things that I have to live with and learn to deal with.

But it is what it is. That's how it all started.

I finished the interview. I assured the social worker I could handle whatever came. I sent her the check and she started her search.

Diane

2009–2010

Winning the Daphne du Maurier Award made a significant impact on my future writing career. One of the judges for the contest was an editor for Harlequin's inspirational romance line, which at that time was called Steeple Hill.

When I received the contest score sheets, I was excited and hugely surprised to discover that the editor had not only given me a perfect score in every category, but she had written a paragraph on the last page telling me how wonderful she thought my writing was and she requested that I send her the completed manuscript for review.

Several months later I received the call that every aspiring writer dreams about. The senior editor, as well as the assistant editor who would be working with me, set up a conference call. They broke the news together that they wanted to publish my first book.

The title of my first manuscript, *Whispers in the Dark*, was changed by the senior editor to *Midnight Caller*. The editor sent me a letter with several revisions she wanted to see and also pointed out some areas she wanted me to expand.

I was now a published author. I had to deal with art fact sheets, back cover blurbs, synopses, revision letters, art suggestions for covers, Dear Reader letters, acknowledgment pages, professional biographies, and my end of marketing and publicity. Then I had to sit my butt in a chair and try to do it all over again.

Life was good. I trusted in the Lord and He continued to bless me.

In March 2010, my first novel hit the store shelves.

Steve

2010–2011

I believe roughly a year and a half had gone by since I had started my search for my mother. Every now and then, I'd check in with the social worker and ask her how it was going. I could tell I was just a file on her desk sometimes because she'd say things like, "Let me revisit your file, see where you're at, and get back to you."

I knew someone wasn't constantly working on my case, and I was okay with that. I had waited thirty-nine or forty-some years by this time and I was trying to be as patient as possible.

I didn't want to be like the kid on Christmas. You know the one. The kid who knows the present is out there, but just can't wait and has to shake the box and find out what's in it. I was trying to keep my emotions and thoughts as controlled as I could.

The whole time this was going on, my step-daughter, Kristin, and my wife, Barb, continued to be very giddy and excited. They continued to watch the show *The Locator*, too. They wanted so much for me to get the answers I was wondering about. They really pushed me into it by constantly telling me, "Call the agency again. You need to find out."

With my personality, I would always downplay it. I would tease them and I'd tell them that I'd heard stuff months ago when I didn't just to get them riled up.

"Did you really?" they'd ask.

"No," I'd say, and we would go on until the next time, sometimes as early as the next episode.

Finally, I called the social worker. Like I said, a full year and a half had gone into the search by that time, so I said, "Okay, so what's the next step? Are you having any luck?"

"Well at this point," Pat said, "I've given up on my end of it. I don't fully believe that I can find your mother. I've exhausted every lead and avenue I have."

I tried hard not to allow myself to feel the huge disappointment her words caused, but I wasn't real successful at it. It's never easy to have your hope taken away.

"But we can go to a private investigator that our agency uses occasionally," she continued.

I felt like I was seeing shiny new bait on the hook, but I bit anyway.

"How does that work?" I asked.

"You send me another check. If he finds her, then you pay the money, but if he doesn't find her, then you get your money back."

I figured that was a pretty low risk opportunity. So I agreed and wrote a second check.

In the meantime, early on in the search process I had received a letter from the adoption agency. It told me very generic stuff about my mother's family and what little they knew about my father.

They told me that my father was of Muslim religion, that he had immigrated to the United States from Jordan. That tidbit of information blew my mind. I'm American born and bred. I wave the flag in my eyes and my heart and my soul and now here I am finding out I have an attachment to a Middle Eastern country and a father who is Muslim. It was really a shock to me.

I looked in the mirror and wondered why I didn't see any Middle Eastern physical characteristics staring back. I would have thought genetically that my father's genes would have dominated. But my skin was milky white. I had medium brown hair, admittedly liberally peppered with gray, and I truly looked more like an Irish leprechaun than a Middle Easterner.

As I calmed down and read through the material again, I discovered that my father's family was originally Russian. They must have immigrated to Jordan. So my dad was of Russian ancestry and Muslim religion and had been raised in a foreign country. That explained my physical appearance, but didn't ease my shock about all the rest.

The whole thing blew my mind because the story I'd been told was that my parents had been two college kids. I had assumed two American college kids. Nobody ever said that one of my parents was from another country.

So that was the first piece of evidence the social worker had warned me about that really shook me to the bone. It was my first hint that this is going to be a wild ride. It didn't look like it was going to be anything normal like I expected it would be. Two college kids. *Yeah, right.*

I had also received the paperwork on my mother. I found out that she was the oldest of seven children. I had six other aunts and uncles out there, probably a ton of cousins and brothers or sisters at some point along the line. So I knew very early on, probably within weeks of that original search process, that I belonged to a huge family.

I didn't have any other information about my father or his family.

On the many evenings I sat on my swing on my back porch and thought about the circumstances of my adoption, the pieces slowly began to fall into place. My mother was Irish Catholic. Having been raised as a Catholic, myself, I had a hunch that that probably was a big piece of my story. I figured my biological parents' different religious beliefs probably led to a rift in their relationship, which I found out later was correct.

In the beginning, because this was the only information I had, I withheld my search from my sons. They knew early on that I'd been adopted, but I didn't tell them about the search because I wanted to give them a complete story instead of teasing them like I was doing to Kristin and Barbara. So I waited. I had some information about my biological parents, but it still wasn't enough for me. I still hadn't gotten the answers I wanted.

If anything, my interest was piqued. Growing up as an only child on a dead end cul-de-sac with no kids around from the age of five to about the age of thirteen, my whole life was isolated. Now I knew I had this huge family out there and I found that pretty exciting.

The only exposure to a family I had had was Barbara's family. Her parents had siblings. Barb had a brother and a sister who both had spouses and kids. So there were brothers and sisters and aunts and uncles and cousins all on her side.

Before the search, I had only had me.

So yeah, I was pretty excited . . . and hopeful . . . and patient. And I'm really glad I was because even though I agreed to hire the private investigator, I didn't get answers right away.

Diane

2010

One of the little idiosyncrasies my husband, Bill, had was collecting discarded pennies. No matter where we went or what we were doing, if he saw a penny lying on the ground, he would pick it up. My father used to tease Bill. He used to say if it were dollar bills maybe he'd bend over for them, but not dirty pennies.

Once on a family trip to Tennessee, my father was walking ahead of us up an incline to Rock City. Bill and I followed a couple yards behind. As we walked up the hill, I noticed my father was dropping pennies one by one like bread crumbs. It caught my attention because his shoulders were shaking from laughing since he knew Bill wouldn't be able to resist picking them up.

Sure enough, Bill did.

"Bill, stop." I pulled on his sleeve. "My father is doing that on purpose to embarrass you."

Bill looked me right in the eye and said, "Darling, if your father is stupid enough to throw away money, then I am smart enough to pick it up."

I never tried to stop Bill from picking up pennies again.

After Bill died, I began finding pennies. They weren't just in parking lots. They were in unusual places like the floor of an elevator after I'd just worked with a particularly difficult patient. Or on the seat of my car, which was unusual because I rarely wear clothes with pockets so I don't know how a penny would get there.

Pennies appeared with frequency and always, always at important times in my life, both good and bad—at my son, David's, wedding or after I'd had a really difficult day. Bright shiny pennies would never be far away.

I used to laugh every time I saw one and I'd always pick it up. After all, I thought if Bill was still watching over me, the least I could do is let him know I appreciated it.

In March 2010, my first book, *Midnight Caller*, was released. I still remember what it felt like to walk into a store for the first time and actually see my book on the shelf. I felt giddy and excited and had to resist the urge to pick up the book and run around showing it to everyone in the place.

My very first book signing was held at a Barnes & Noble in Melbourne, Florida, about an hour and a half from my home. I was nervous as I took the trip. I imagined how embarrassing it would be if I found myself sitting at a table in the middle of the store while people walked past me without a second glance. I was equally as nervous as I thought about what I'd say and what I'd sign if someone really did approach me with a copy of my book.

As I was driving up to the store, my thoughts strayed to Bill. He would have been so proud of me.

"Thank you, God, for making this dream come true. I am so grateful for this blessing," I prayed aloud. "Please, please let Bill know."

When I pulled up in the parking lot, I stood on the sidewalk and just stared. In the window of the Barnes & Noble was a large picture of my book cover and right next to it was an equally large picture of me. I was speechless. You'd think I was somebody special. *If they only knew . . .*

When I entered the store, I found a table had been set up for me to the right of the entrance where everyone entering or exiting the store would see me. To my amazement, two people were already standing in line waiting for me. Balloons were attached to the edge of the table. My books were neatly stacked up in two piles. Right next to the books were a pen and a cold bottle of water.

I said hello to the people in line and hurried around the table. I froze for a good thirty seconds before I sat down. In the middle of the table, on that beautiful white tablecloth, was a bright, shiny penny.

Chapter

10

Steve

2011–2012

Even after the private investigator was on the case, multiple months went by and I still didn't hear anything.

The more time that passed, both my wife and Kristin became almost silly and hostile. They were constantly asking me if I'd heard anything. My wife would bang around the kitchen saying, "I'm going to call that woman. She isn't doing her job. You should have heard something by now."

I'd respond, "Just calm down. I'm not going to rush this."

They were very much in a this-has-to-be-done-yesterday mindset. I was not like that at all. I'd waited forty-some years. What was another couple of months? It really wasn't going to make that much of a difference. In my mind, the search had begun and that was the most important thing.

But time kept passing.

Money gets tight every now and then for most people. I'm no exception. The money I had sent to the private investigator was tied up and not producing any results. Finally, I said to Barb, "You know, I'm gonna give it two more weeks. If I don't hear anything, I'm going to tell Pat to return my check and we'll use the money for expenses around the house."

I never planned on dropping the search for my mother completely. I fully intended to gear back up down the road and find a private investigator on my own, who, I might add, would have had to give me the information on my mother even if my mother didn't want to be contacted.

I wouldn't have pushed contacting her, though. I'd already promised myself that I would not disrupt anyone's life. But I would probably still be able to track down pictures of her on the Internet and do research on my own without making contact. Whether she wanted to know about me, I still wanted to see who she was. I wanted to know what she looked like. I wanted to know where she lived. I wanted to try to find answers for all those questions that have rattled around inside my mind for years.

If that's all it ever was, I could have lived with that.

But we didn't get to that point because within days of making that statement to my wife, I received a phone call at work from the social worker. Pat was almost crying on the phone. "He found her. He found your mother."

I was surprisingly very stoic, very non-emotional. Through this entire process, I did not allow myself to give in to my emotions. I controlled myself, probably because I didn't want to get hurt. Nobody had made contact with my mother yet, so we still didn't know how she'd react or if she would want anything to do with me. Rejection was only a telephone call away. So I held my emotions very close to the vest.

"We are 100 percent sure it's her," Pat assured me.

"How can you be so sure? Can I ask that?" I was hoping she'd give me one more clue to my mother's identity just in case my mother closed the door on her end.

"We found her through public records. The private investigator found the names of your mother's siblings in the record and it matched everything we had in our files on your family background perfectly."

I couldn't get any other information from her. The agency was very secretive since it had been a closed adoption and my mother hadn't signed any of the release papers yet.

"Okay, what happens now?" I asked.

Now that they had an address, they were going to send out three letters. The first letter was going to be a generic letter stating there was an important family matter to discuss and we'd like her to contact us. If she didn't respond to the first letter, then they would send a second letter that would have a little more teaser information in it.

If still no response, then the third letter would be sent certified. If the first two letters had been thrown away—maybe by an angry husband, maybe by my mother herself because she didn't know what it was, or even maybe because my mother *did* know and wasn't ready to deal with it—at least I'd know without doubt that she'd have to sign for this one so she'd definitely received it.

And that's what happened.

Diane

April 10, 2012

Confused, upset, I gripped the phone and waited for Pat Fowler to tell me what this was all about.

In a soft, gentle voice, Ms. Fowler asked, "Mrs. Burke, did you give up a child for adoption in 1971?"

Those words played over and over in my mind. *Oh my God, I can't believe it. This couldn't be happening. Not after all these years.*

"Yes," I whispered, my voice laced with tears.

"Mrs. Burke, I am not trying to upset you. I simply want to know if you'd be willing to answer some medical questions for me for the file."

Medical questions? Of course, what else had I expected? They just needed to update their files in case my son ever needs it.

"Of course," I said.

I tried to hide my disappointment. I'd thought . . . maybe . . . just maybe . . .

We spent the next few minutes discussing the necessary health backgrounds of myself, my parents, and my siblings. The whole time I was relating the information in as calm a voice as I could muster, my heart hammered in my chest so hard it almost hurt. My mind raced with a hundred questions and a thousand memories.

Don't get excited. It's just the agency updating their files. It's not like your son is asking about you.

"That about does it, Mrs. Burke. Thank you for your time and information."

"You're welcome."

So that's that. See? Clerical information. That's all anybody wanted. Now let it go, Diane.

"Mrs. Burke, can I have just one more moment of your time?" Her voice sounded tentative but determined.

When I agreed, she continued, "I've come to know your son and he is a very nice young man."

Tears welled up again and my vision blurred so much I couldn't see.

"He's been searching for you for over three years," she said.

Oh my God!

"When we were unable to locate you," Pat said, "We used a private investigator that often works with our agency in a last attempt to turn something up."

A private investigator?

The first smile of the day teased my lips. My son must have really wanted to find me.

"When the investigator found you, we sent out a letter to you immediately."

"What letter? I never received a letter."

"We sent it, Mrs. Burke. In the letter we asked you to contact us."

"That can't be. I never got any letter." What was happening? I'd never received a letter. I wouldn't have forgotten getting a bombshell letter like that one would have been.

Pat's voice remained soft and gentle, although this time I could hear a slight tinge of scolding. "We sent it, Mrs. Burke. A few months later we sent a second letter as well."

Two letters?

"I don't understand. I never got any letters." My mind raced. "I would have called you immediately if I had gotten a letter."

"Our records show they were sent."

"Did you have the name of the adoption agency as the return address?"

"No. We don't do that for privacy reasons. The return address would simply have been our street address, nothing more."

"I don't understand. I don't remember ever getting any letter from you, let alone two."

"Maybe you mistook them for junk mail and threw them away. Do you open your junk mail?"

"No. I just toss the envelopes in the trash."

Is that what I did? Did I throw away the chance to learn about my son not just once, but twice?

What if this letter hadn't come certified? It had said it would be the last attempt to reach me. My stomach clenched into a painful knot.

"That's what you must have done, then." Pat's voice sounded happier now that she suspected I had thrown it away as junk rather than ignored it or just hadn't replied.

"Can you tell me about him?" I wanted to know everything and anything that she was willing to share. She was talking about my *son*. This was so surreal. It was three months shy of forty-one years. How could this be happening?

"Yes, I can. He has already signed all of the release papers. His name is Steve. He works in a warehouse and drives a fork-lift. But his job is more complicated than it sounds. This particular job was not easy to get. Your son works very hard and works under stressful conditions but he is compensated well and has been at this job for several years. His title is Warehouse Specialist."

My smile widened as I remembered working in a factory with his father. Watching his father jump between machines, trying to fix them when they broke down.

"He's married. Has been married almost nineteen years. He has three step-children, two of the older children are adults now and live in New Jersey, one step-daughter lives with him and is attending college, and he has two sons. Steven is the oldest and Kevin is a year younger."

I have more grandchildren. My heart leapt with anticipation and joy.

I'm sure I said something inane, something stupid like, "That's nice." All I really remember doing was crying.

"He doesn't want to cause any problems for you. He doesn't want to interfere in your life in any way."

My throat constricted and I couldn't speak. I merely waited for her to continue.

"But I promised your son that I'd ask . . ." She paused, as if she were waiting for me to give her permission to continue.

"Ask?"

"Mrs. Burke, your son asked me, if I actually had the chance to talk to you, to ask if you would be willing to talk to him on the phone just once. He told me that he will understand and he won't bother you anymore if you say no."

Before I could reply or do anything more than cry, Pat started talking really fast. "He also asked if you were open to a phone call from him that maybe there might be a chance you might be willing to meet him face-to-face just once . . . and if you would be willing to do that, would it be possible for him to bring his family with him?"

Now I was sobbing, deep, gut-wrenching, moaning sobs.

"Mrs. Burke . . . Are you all right?"

"Yes!" My smile was so wide, it barely fit my face. "Yes! Yes! Yes to everything! Please, tell me how I can talk to my son."

Pat's voice sounded as happy as I felt. "Well, he's at work right now and with the kind of job he does, he's not usually able to take calls so it probably wouldn't be a good idea for you to call him at work."

I nodded like she could see me through the phone.

"But I'll contact him and tell him that you'd like to talk to him and see what I can set up."

"I never wanted to give him up," I said. "Make sure he knows that. Make sure he knows I can't wait to talk to him and I just can't believe this is happening."

Pat laughed some more. "I'll contact him now and try to get back to you in just a few minutes."

Chapter

11

Steve

After the first letter from the agency went out, I thought for sure I'd probably hear something within the first two weeks. I was thinking that if my mother truly wanted to have a conversation with me or contact with me, then as soon as she got that letter, she probably would have raced to the phone to call the number.

When the first month went by, that's when negative emotions began to creep in. For the first time in my life, I began to think about being unwanted, about being rejected. Those thoughts had never really crossed my mind before. I was beginning to realize that maybe I was going to be disappointed at the end of this search. I mean, there was no way she *didn't* get a letter. Everybody gets a letter in the mail. What are the odds that this letter, maybe one of the most important letters of my life, got lost?

Then the second letter went out.

Pat called me and told me exactly when she was mailing that second letter, and I kept an eye on the calendar and my ear waiting for a call on the phone. Then another month or two went by with no response.

I was two to three months into this thing *after* they'd found her and had received no response whatsoever. I was really starting to believe those negative thoughts. I began to believe she wanted nothing to do with me. While all this was going on, my wife and step-daughter were going around saying, "Well, that's her loss 'cause you're a terrific guy. She doesn't know."

Of course, I couldn't care less about that. I don't want to raise myself up on a platform, saying that I'm a great guy or not a great guy—whatever, that's for other people to judge.

But those feelings of rejection, those feelings that your *mother*, probably one of the most important and definitely the very first relationship in your life, didn't want you—even though I'd been warned, it was still a bitter pill to swallow.

Then the certified letter went out.

I was satisfied. I figured at least one way or the other I was going to have closure because she would have had to sign for the letter. If there was still no personal response from my mother, then there'd be no question anymore about how she felt.

Within days of sending that certified letter, I got a phone call from the social worker while I was out in the parking lot on my lunch break. Pat informed me that not only did my mother sign for the letter, but that she called right away, couldn't wait to talk to me, and that she wanted me to know that she had never wanted to give me up.

My whole world changed that afternoon.

I was ecstatic, but still very reserved. I was probably numb more than anything. From the time I was six years old, the questions had slowly crept in and grew harder to ignore as I got older and older. You're talking about thirty-four years of knowing that your parents are your parents, but, then again, they're not. Your family is your family but isn't really.

When you become an adult and can analyze the situation, those questions become a challenge to your intellect. Who am I? Where do I belong? What is my nationality? Who are my family? What was the situation that caused my adoption in the first place? All those things, every question that an adopted child could possibly come up with, all those questions that had been building up for the past thirty-four years, were now just a phone call away from being answered.

It was almost like being in a dream.

At that point, the social worker had set up a phone call for seven o'clock that night between my mother and me. Within just a few hours, I would no longer live in a fantasy world.

That's how I used to describe my life to people: it was a fantasy world. I would look at my brother-in-law and my wife and my friends and I would say, "You all know who your mothers are. You've had your mothers from the time you were infants. Can you imagine being a forty-year-old man and never knowing who your mother is? Not knowing who your brothers or your sisters are? Not knowing who your grandparents were? Not knowing where you were supposed to live or who you were supposed to be?"

I always felt alone.

I really truly believe this contributed to my personality, of my being a solitary type of person in a lot of ways. It was always just me. I was the only true link to that parallel life before these answers came. I am not a true Orlandi, but I just didn't know who I was.

I was myself. And that's all I knew.

People have a hard time imagining what it was like to be me. To be three months short of forty-one and yet have never met your mom. It's crazy.

People who aren't adoptees and don't go through it can't relate. If you've had your mother from Day One, if she's taken care of you when you were sick, when you had a scraped knee, or any of the million other things that mothers do, then you gradually grow into loving your mother and knowing everything there is to know about her. You arrive at my age with a life-long history between the two of you.

Not me.

I was going to talk to my mother for the first time that night at seven o'clock. I didn't even know at forty-years-old what my mother's voice sounded like. Can you imagine that? All those questions were going to be answered at seven o'clock.

So, again, I settled in to wait.

Diane

After the social worker hung up, I stared at the phone while I waited for her to get back to me about setting up a phone call that night. My son wanted to talk to me. My son had been looking for me for more than three years. My son wanted to meet me.

Thank you, Lord. From the bottom of my heart, thank you. This is more than I ever asked for. This is more than I ever believed could be.

Even though I'd been staring at it, when the phone rang it startled me and I grabbed it right away.

"Steve wants to know if you can call him at his home tonight at seven o'clock?" Pat asked.

I agreed. She gave me his telephone number.

Then she asked, "Mrs. Burke, I'm not at liberty to give him any information that I have about you because you haven't signed any of the release papers. But is there anything you want me to tell him? I'm sure he's anxious to know something. What would you like me to say? How would you describe yourself?"

What did I want to say? How could I summarize almost forty-one years in ten seconds? What did I want my son to know about me?

"Tell him that I had a hard life with many challenges. Tell him that I put myself through college at the age of forty. That I am a published author. That I worked hard to turn my life around and that I am very proud of the person that I have become." I paused for a second and considered if there was anything else I wanted to say. "Pat, tell him that I am a survivor."

"I'll tell him."

Before she could hang up, I stopped her. "Oh, and Pat, at least tell him my first name is Diane. I wouldn't want him to think I'm a telemarketer when I call and have him hang up on me."

"I'll tell him." I could hear the smile in her voice. "I hope the call goes well. And remember, we are here to help. If there is anything we can do to make this easier for either of you, please let us know and we'll be happy to try and help."

"Thank you."

I hung up the phone and almost danced around my bedroom. Then, I picked up the phone and started dialing every living soul I knew. Of course, I began with my other two sons. To say they were astounded that their brother had contacted me is an understatement. I can truthfully say both of them were very happy for me because they knew how much it meant to me. They'd been eyewitnesses to my sense of loss and pain all their lives.

Then I settled in to wait.

I was going to talk to my long lost son.

Tonight.

In less than seven hours, I would hear the grown up voice of the baby I had last seen in the arms of a nurse as he was carried out of my hospital room.

My son had found me. He had cared enough to search and he had found me.

I stared hard at the hands of the clock and spent the rest of the afternoon trying to will the time to fly.

Steve

That five- or six-hour stretch at work, which I still say was the longest day of my life, was unbelievable. The reality of the situation was almost overwhelming. I didn't cry. I didn't even allow myself to get euphoric and emotional and happy. I was just . . . there. I had no emotions left because this was so important, so mind-blowing, that I didn't know how to handle it.

How do you handle it?

How do you handle being forty years old and knowing you're going to talk to your mother for the first time in your life? How many people in the world go through that? Certainly a very small percentage. Although I know there are a lot of adoptees out there, the majority of the population is not adopted.

My wife, Barb, was ecstatic. She texted everybody ever listed in her phone and *then* asked me if she could text anybody else. I laughed and told her to text the world. I was at work, where I have hardly any time for any personal stuff, and my phone was pinging away from all the texts coming in from my in-laws and my friends. I did approach two of my best buddies at work and told them that my mother made contact. All in all, it was a crazy, communicative day.

The social worker had also told me I had two brothers, which is something that I had always wondered about, and that information was going around inside my head, too. A whole new world was opening up for me. I remember thinking, *Like it or not, here it comes.* I had gone from being myself alone in this world to being a member of a family—my DNA, my blood, my clan—in just one afternoon.

⊙ ❈ ⊙

I did a terrible thing to Barb and Kristin that night. This was April 10. They had been up in New Jersey the beginning of the month and had just recently come home. When I came in the door, they were both excited and happy as they anticipated tonight's call. The second I walked in the door, I grinned at them and said, "April Fools'! Ha, ha, ha. Just 'cause you weren't here doesn't mean you get out of being fooled." Then I headed upstairs to take a shower.

I have a wicked sense of humor and I tease the people I love unmercifully. This was one of those times and it was driving both of the girls nuts. Because I pull pranks all the time, they weren't sure which one was the prank. Was I really going to talk to my mother that night? Or was it a not-so-funny April Fools' joke? I could hear them downstairs freaking out, knowing I was pulling a fast one but honestly not sure which one. The more time that passed, the more upset they became.

Mean? Sure, but also a heck of a lot of fun. I could hear them from upstairs and I was laughing my butt off. In hindsight, I think that joke just might have been a way for me to relieve some of my own stress, maybe to show the world, even myself, that this wasn't really any big deal when, in truth, it was the biggest deal in the world to me.

I was going to speak to my mother.

Downstairs, Barb and Kristin were doing everything they could think of to figure things out. They tried checking my cell phone to see if any of the recent numbers were from the social worker. They kept talking between themselves, weighing the pros and cons to whether I would have encouraged them to text the entire family for just a silly prank. When they realized I was home fifteen minutes early, they finally put the pieces together. I am a creature of habit. I like routine and order in my life and I rarely step from it. Coming home early gave them their answer. By the time I'd come back downstairs, they were armed and ready.

"You're lying," Barb accused.

"You are getting a call, aren't you?" Kristin asked, in an equally accusing tone.

I nudged past both of them and said, "Can't talk with you right now. I have to get out to my swing so I'll be ready when my mother calls."

To this day, we still get a good laugh out of that one.

⚜

What was I going to say on the phone? I played with it all day long. How was I going to greet my mother? I knew her name was Diane. So the easiest thing would have been to say "Hello, Diane," but I remembered what the social worker had told me, that my mother was excited about being able to talk to me, that she'd never wanted to give me up. Those were very important things that my mother had wanted me to know right away.

Having that information, I assumed my mother might be open to a different greeting. I knew what I wanted to say. I just kept second-guessing myself as to whether it was a good idea.

Diane

I spent the afternoon calling every living relative and friend I had and my voice was already getting hoarse. As seven o'clock approached, I sat at my computer desk and alternated between staring at the phone and staring at the clock. At exactly seven,

I dialed. He answered the phone before the end of the first ring.

"Hello?"

"Is this Steve?"

"Yes."

"Hello, Steve. This is Diane."

"Hello, Mom."

A floodgate of tears burst from my eyes and my body literally shook with sobs. I was crying so hard, I almost missed the next thing he said.

"It's so good to hear your voice after all these years."

This deep, rich, warm, masculine voice on the other end of the line was my son. I couldn't believe it was truly happening.

My memory is sketchy about what we talked about. Everything important and nothing important. I remember giving him a synopsis of the events that had led to the adoption and that was probably the heaviest part of the conversation. The rest of the conversation covered topics like what state I currently lived in and where was I born and was I a cat person or a dog person?

On his end, he told me all about his job and I soon discovered that Pat hadn't been kidding. It was much more complicated than simply operating a fork lift. He told me about his wife, Barbara, and there was no question by the things he said and the loving tone in his voice when he talked about her that even nineteen years later, he was still madly in love with his wife.

He told me about his children and his step-children. That Kevin loved hockey and was a Flyers fan. That Steven was going to graduate from high school in six weeks. That, although the other step-children were grown and living in New Jersey, Kristin was still living with them and attending college.

We talked about everything and anything and it was wonderful.

Almost two-and-a-half hours later, I said, "Steve, I'm so sorry but I have to hang up. I'm so hoarse, I can hardly speak another word."

"I understand. Would you mind if I call you again?"

I laughed. "I'd mind if you didn't."

He chuckled, too. "Okay, how about seven o'clock tomorrow night?"

"Seven it is."

Steve did call me at seven. He called me at seven o'clock the next night and every night after that for months. He still calls me three or four times a week, even now after the newness of our relationship has worn off. We miss our calls only when life gets in the way and he has something else he has to do or someplace he has to go.

Sometimes the calls are brief. How was your day? How are you feeling? Just short calls to touch base with one another. Sometimes the calls go on for hours. We laugh and joke and tease one another. He's easy to talk to—witty, sarcastic, intelligent— and I truly enjoy our phone conversations.

I say prayers of thanksgiving every night. God knows that I consider myself amply blessed because this witty, sarcastic, intelligent man is my son, and he has finally come home.

Chapter

12

Diane

The next few days passed in a haze. I'm sure my feet never touched the ground. I was happier than I thought humanly possible and all I wanted to do now was see my grown son face-to-face. I spoke to Steve on the phone for hours on Tuesday and again on Wednesday and Thursday. I was already thinking about driving up to meet him and his family.

My brother was the voice of reason. He kept telling me to slow down, not do anything right now. He didn't want me to appear to be a stalker or an emotionally needy person who might scare Steve away. He kept reminding me, too, that although this whole situation was wonderful and Steve sounded like a nice guy, he was still a stranger.

My brother told me I should play it cool and let him come to me. That maybe we could plan something in the near future where Steve and his family could come to Florida. Then my brother and his family, as well as my son, Dan, and his family, would be present when Steve and I met. He thought that scenario would make it easier and less awkward for everybody.

Logically, that made perfect sense.

Emotionally, I wasn't so sure.

Steve and I really hit it off on the phone. We could talk to each other for hours as though we had been with one another our entire lives. Deep inside, I really thought he'd want to see me as much as I wanted to see him. And, boy, did I want to see him.

Wednesday morning, when I went on Facebook to check my updates, I discovered that Steve had posted about how wonderful it had been to talk to me on the phone and how happy he was to have finally talked to his mother. It was a beautiful posting. Perusing Steve's Facebook site, I also discovered that he and his family were planning to come to Florida in July.

Wednesday night, I decided to call Steve and thank him for the lovely posting. Barb answered the phone.

"I'm sorry to bother you," I said, "And I promise that I won't be calling you every night and driving you crazy but . . ."

She immediately interrupted me. "You are Steve's mother. You can call this house whenever and as often as you like."

"Thanks. I appreciate that."

Barb was so sweet. When I later discovered that she and her daughter, Kristin, had been the driving forces throughout the search, I was surprised at the amount of encouragement and support she'd provided my son. After I got to know her better, though, I was no longer surprised; she understood how important it was to Steve to find his mother and she loves him.

"I was wondering if I could talk to Steve," I said. "I wanted to thank him for the lovely post he placed about me on Facebook."

"He just got in from work. He's in the shower. I'll have him call you as soon as he gets out."

"Okay, fine. Listen, I saw that your family is planning a vacation on Sanibel Island in July. I was wondering if maybe we could arrange to meet somewhere while you're here."

"What are you, crazy?" she asked with her heavy New Jersey Italian accent.

Uh-oh! Maybe my brother was right. I was moving too fast and blowing it.

"Steve's been looking for you for over three years," Barbara said. "Do you really think he's going to wait until July to meet you now that he's found you? You have to come up with something earlier than that."

I laughed out loud.

"Good," I said. "Well, then, what would you think of me driving up there this weekend and surprising him?"

"What?!" Barbara sounded so excited and happy. "You'd do that?"

"If Steve can search for me for three years, the least I can do is drive a few hours to see him."

"Oh my god, he'll die! He'll fall on the floor! That would be wonderful, but I'll never be able to keep it a secret."

"Oh, Barb, please, you have to. Think how great it will be if we can pull this off."

"Okay, I'll try, but you don't know Steve. This isn't going to be an easy-to-keep secret."

So our plan was launched. When Steve called that night, I didn't give any indication I would be seeing him soon. I'm glad we were on a regular phone and not Skype, though, because if he could have seen the wide open grin on my face during the whole phone conversation, he would have known something was up.

Thursday morning I set things in motion. Getting my hair cut and colored so I'd look my best. Getting an oil change and a couple of new tires so I'd feel safe in my old clunker automobile. Arranging my work schedule so I could have the next day off.

Everything was going smoothly until my ex-husband, Danny, who had become a friend over the years, told my youngest son, David, what I was planning to do.

Then the phone calls started.

"Mom, you can't drive your car there. It's got 168,000 miles on it. What if it breaks down on the side of the road?"

"I have AAA."

"Great. So they tow you to the nearest repair shop. Then what?"

"Okay, so I won't drive my car. I'll rent a car," I replied, and a lengthy conversation about what kind of car and what car rental company to use ensued.

"Look, you haven't been feeling well lately, I know your stomach has been bothering you," Dave said. "What if you get sick?"

"I'll be fine, David, stop worrying."

"It's a long drive for you, Mom. Are you sure you can do it on your own?"

'Yes, I can do it on my own. Stop worrying."

The day passed in a blur of last-minute errands and activities when I got David's final telephone call early that evening.

"Hi, Mom."

"Yes, David?"

"Don't rent a car."

"Why not? I've just left a car rental agency and arranged to pick one up in the morning."

"Well, don't, because I rented one for us. I'm at the Daytona Beach airport and should be at your place in about twenty minutes."

"What?" I couldn't believe what I was hearing. He had flown in from Virginia.

"Don't sound so surprised. Did you really think I was going to let you drive all that way by yourself? What if something happens on the road? And I'm not going to let you walk into a stranger's house alone. Besides, I want to meet my brother, too."

I was deeply touched that David was going to all this trouble for me and, truthfully, very glad for the company. The older I get, the harder it is making long drives.

Then I started getting calls from Barbara.

"We've got a problem," she whispered.

"What?" My heart sped up and now I started to worry. "Why are you whispering?"

"Because I'm standing in my closest so Steve doesn't hear me on the phone with you."

"What's the problem?"

"He's coming to you."

"What?" I was in shock.

"He called me and told me he was taking Friday off from work and we were going to drive down there for the weekend."

"What did you say to him?"

"I told him that I couldn't get Friday off. He questioned it, at first, because he knows I can pretty much take any time I need off, but I told him that there was a big staff meeting that day and I couldn't miss it."

"Well, it sounds like you handled it well."

"Not really. He told me he took Monday off. He called to put the dogs in the kennel. I had to call the kennel after he did and tell them we'd changed our minds. They probably think I'm crazy."

Both of us laughed hysterically.

"I've never lied to my husband in nineteen years as much as I've lied to him in the past twenty-four hours," Barb said.

I laughed again. "Well, stop lying. Let me lie to him. Tell him he should call me tonight and make sure that I'll be home this weekend before he makes the trip. I'll do the rest."

Like clockwork, Steve called at seven.

"Mom, I was wondering if you would mind if Barb and I came down for the weekend? Don't worry. We wouldn't expect to crash at your house or anything. I looked it up online and there are plenty of hotels in your area. I was just thinking that maybe we could grab a cup of coffee or lunch or something and meet in person."

I could hear the hopefulness in his voice and I felt really bad about what I was about to do.

"Oh, Steve," I said. "I'm so sorry. I won't be home this weekend. I am attending a writer's conference down in south Florida. Normally, I'd gladly cancel, but I'm teaching one of the classes and I can't. They've had it set up for months."

"I understand."

I could hardly bear the deep disappointment I heard in his voice.

"Well, when can I come?" he asked. "I have other obligations the next two weekends but then I'm free."

"My brother, Michael, and his family will be coming to Florida for vacation around May 19. Why don't you plan on coming then? You'll get to meet two of your uncles and their families and probably one of your brothers and his family, too."

A long, heavy silence filled the airwaves.

"Okay," Steve said. "I've waited forty years to meet you. I guess I can wait five more weeks."

My heart broke for him, but I was grinning from ear to ear. This surprise visit was going to be awesome!

Steve

Friday the thirteenth arrived. I am not a superstitious person. I don't freak out if a black cat crosses in front of me. I'm not afraid of walking under ladders. And I definitely never gave Friday the thirteenth a second thought as anything other than the title of a bad teen horror flick. But I won't ever forget it now. For me, it will always be one of the luckiest days of my life.

By Friday, after several lengthy phone calls with my mother, I knew I had two brothers. My mother had told me that both brothers were very happy and excited that I was back on the scene. A flurry of Facebook friend requests and confirmations occurred while everybody was scurrying to get an even better peek into each other's lives.

That's the best gift that Facebook has ever given me. I was able to see pictures of my mother and both my brothers instantly when I got off the phone that very first night. I have to chuckle because I know my mother ran to Facebook that night, too, to see what her son and her grandchildren looked like as well.

I friended one brother, Dan, and he never responded. I friended the younger brother, Dave, and he responded right away with a message welcoming me to the family.

The second night on the phone, my mother told me that my brother, Dan, had pulled back a bit and was going to do this a bit more cautiously, which I completely respected. Like I've said earlier, the last thing I ever intended to do was disrupt anybody's life. Whether I liked it or not, I understood that everybody had a life of their own for forty or so years without me in it, and I had to be respectful of that fact. But this was unknown territory for all of us, including me, and it wasn't easy.

Adoption reunions do nothing but disrupt lives. No matter if the reunions are perceived to be good, bad, or indifferent, they're going to disrupt lives. So that's the responsibility, or maybe the cross, that I had to bear, knowing I was knocking at a door that some people may not want to answer.

I heard back from David right away. He was ecstatic. He was so thrilled and he told me that he felt blessed that his big brother was back in his life. He told me he'd known about me for years, but he had never really believed he would ever have the opportunity to meet me.

His message made me feel welcome and put me at ease. I fired a message back saying I was equally as thrilled to find out I had a baby brother, which is something I had hoped was true since my teens.

I was still waiting for a response from Dan, who seemed to be taking a "let's just wait and see where this thing goes" approach. I can say now that I've gotten to know him that I find I am very much like him. I am also a cautious individual, particularly when it comes to anything that would involve my wife and my kids, and I like to know that whatever situation I present them with is as safe and controlled as possible. So his hesitancy to friending me on Facebook was not an insult in any way, but it was a disappointment.

That first week after I'd spoken to my mother for the first time, I was riding a roller coaster of emotions. I experienced the high of one brother acting really, really excited and then the low of the other brother kind of pulling back. As conservative as I had been through the whole process, I had discovered that I wanted to make instant contact with all three of them—my mother and both brothers. So when Dan pulled back, it affected me. I don't really know what word to use to describe how I was feeling at that moment. Perturbed? Annoyed? It surprised me a little bit in a negative way because why, after your long lost brother has found you, wouldn't you want to rush right in and greet him like you see on the television shows?

But life isn't a television show, is it?

As the days and weeks unfolded, my mom would explain more and more to me about the family dynamics. She went into more detail about the problems my brothers had gone through, what the family had gone through, and specifically what my mother had gone through, and I realized what a hard life they had had. It put into perspective why Dan wanted to take it slow, and I was able to completely understand his reservations.

But since I didn't know these things in those first couple days, I guess I was feeling a little bit stung at the time.

I definitely was having mixed feelings that Friday, the thirteenth.

I had had a particularly hard day at work. People had called in sick and my work load had doubled so I was hot, sweaty, and exhausted when I pulled up in the driveway.

I had seen on Facebook that my brother, Dave, and his wife, Esther, had recently been visiting her family in India and Dubai. I sent him several messages after his initial welcome message to me, but he hadn't responded to any of them. I couldn't help but wonder if his trip out of the country was the reason or if it was something else.

I still had no response from my brother, Dan.

Then trying to get down to meet my mom on the weekend only to find out she had other plans—which I totally under-stood. After all, I'd contacted her for the first time on Tuesday, and this was Friday. She had a life, and who was I to come in and mess it up?

But . . . all three things had started my mind down an uncomfortable path.

My brother, Dan, was still missing in action. My brother, Dave, who had been so excited and enthusiastic was suddenly silent. My mother was busy—or was she? I couldn't help but wonder if something else was going on. You know, what sales-people call buyer's remorse? You get all happy about a pur-chase and then you get home and second-guess yourself and wonder if the purchase was a mistake.

Those thoughts tormented me at the time. Were these excuses legitimate, or was my newfound family feeling "buyer's remorse"? Should I gear up for some hurt and rejection?

The last thing in the world I expected on that Friday was what I got.

I was tired. I had had a tough day at work. My mind wasn't on a potential surprise visit from *anybody*. I was still thinking that David wasn't even in this country from his visit abroad and my mother was on her way to southern Florida for a writer's conference.

When I opened that door and saw my mother and brother standing there waiting for me I was shocked. I didn't get emotional or shed any tears or anything. I was literally, to my bones, shocked.

From Tuesday to Friday, I'd gone from finding out for the first time that my mother was still alive and that my brother even existed, to coming home three days later and finding them standing in my kitchen.

Yeah, I was shocked and numb.

The first thing I can remember thinking is, *Oh my God, I can't believe they made the trip to come and see me*. I was also astounded that my wife wasn't just in on it, but that she'd been able to keep it a secret. (Everybody who knows me knows I'm usually a nosebag and can find out everything.)

A quick look around the room revealed that my two sons were also there. My stepdaughter was crying and my wife's eyes were filled with tears. I saw how happy everybody was for me.

I'm not really the kind of person who suffers from a loss of words very often. Truthfully, I'm not shy about sharing my opinions and can sometimes be a bit too blunt when I do. But this day, on this particular Friday, I was at a complete loss.

As my mother wrapped her arms around me and I hugged her back, I was speechless. I was hugging my mother for the first time!

Thankfully, my family recorded the meeting so I'll have a video to always remind me, as if I'd ever forget. It was an awesome, awesome day. What can I say? Hugging my mother and my brother. Holding both their hands in mine, I took my rightful place in the middle of the chain—a chain that had been broken for decades and was now complete.

Yeah, I was at a loss for words. I will never forget that moment for as long as I live. It was one of the highlights of my life, right up there with my marriage to Barb and the birth of my sons. We had the most fantastic weekend ever.

It worked out better than any television show ever could.

Chapter

13

Diane

My brother is usually right. But, thankfully, not this time. The weekend I surprised Steve couldn't have turned out better and was one of the happiest times of my life.

Barbara had invited both David and I to stay with her, but I respectfully declined and we stayed at a nearby hotel. She arranged to meet me at the hotel and drive me to their house about an hour before Steve came home from work. She knew if Steve saw a car with Florida plates anywhere on the block, he'd be suspicious and the surprise would be ruined.

I'm sure she was as nervous about meeting me for the first time as I was about meeting her, but it was totally unnecessary. I recognized her the second she got out of her car. When Barb and Kristin walked into the lobby, I went over to introduce myself. I don't remember who hugged who first. Who cares? All I know is that, within seconds, we were wrapped in each other's arms. From that moment to this one, we have been blessed to be not just in-laws but true, heart-felt family as well as friends.

Dave, who had run up to the room for a moment, joined us. A few more introductions and we were on our way.

Their home was beautiful. It sat on a lovely, heavily wooded property. It had a long, sloping driveway. As we approached the drive, my breath caught in my throat and a tear or two burned my eyes. The similarity hit me like I had just walked into an invisible wall and I needed a second or two to recover: the color was different and it wasn't a split level, but this house—it's heavily treed grounds, it's sloping driveway, it's size—reminded me so much of another house, the house in Kinnelon, New Jersey, where I'd lived when I graduated from high school. The house I lived in when I met Steve's father. The house I left as a pregnant teenager and returned to as a grieving mother.

My thoughts flashed to my mother. I strongly felt her presence and wondered what she was making of all this.

We entered the house through the garage. The door opened into the kitchen and within seconds a teenage boy, just about eye level with me, appeared. He was bouncing around a bit and grinning from ear to ear.

"Hi. My name's Kevin."

I hugged him and was surprised to feel his entire body quivering with excitement. I had to chuckle. Nobody had ever been that happy to meet me before and I loved every second of it.

A minute or two after that, a tall young man, a bit more reserved than his brother, approached and introduced himself. "I'm Steven."

I hugged him, too.

This entire situation seemed like a dream and I didn't want to wake up. I was standing in the kitchen of my son's house with his wife, stepdaughter, and sons. I was meeting my family—*my family*—for the first time since I'd watched my baby carried out of my hospital room.

God's hand was all over this and I felt truly blessed.

Thank God I chose life over abortion.

Thank God I gave Steve the chance to live and love and have a family of his own.

My path, my individual road, had not been easy and had been filled with its share of pain. But God was giving me a chance to see that by not taking the easy way out, by giving my child a chance at life, it all worked out in the end.

Standing with David, Barb, Kristin, Kevin, and Steven, I anticipated the arrival of my son, Steve. I was almost over the moon with happiness. I knew with certainty that if I could go back in time, I would make the same decision for life all over again. The only word I can use to describe what I felt in that moment is *joy*.

The family knew before I did that Steve was home. The excitement level increased tenfold. Everybody scrambled to grab their cameras and get their videos set to go. Lots of "Shhh, shhh, he'll hear us" was whispered around the kitchen.

Barbara suggested I stand just a little bit inside the door so that I would be the first person he'd see when he opened it. Dave stood right behind me. The rest of the family huddled in the kitchen area, cameras poised and ready.

Steve has a routine. When he enters the garage, he empties his ice packs out of his lunch box and sticks them in the freezer to reset for the next day. He leaves his lunch box on top of his tool bench. He takes his cell phone off his belt. Then, he gets out his wallet and his keys and heads into the house.

The entire routine takes a minute, maybe a minute and a half, but on that day, as we waited inside the kitchen, it felt like time had literally stopped and inside the kitchen we were going crazy.

Finally, Steve opened the door, stepped inside, and froze. He actually shook his head from side to side—like when people in movies see a ghost and they think maybe they're imagining things. He just stood there. He didn't move. He didn't speak. He just stared at me.

More time passed.

I couldn't stand it anymore and I rushed toward him.

I said, "Hello, Steve." Then I kissed him on the cheek and threw my arms around him. He fumbled to reach out and drop his keys on the counter and then he hugged me back. I could feel his arms holding me tight. I could feel his face buried in my neck. I was overcome with emotion and joy.

I didn't cry. I was so happy, it would have been virtually impossible to manufacture a tear at that moment. All I knew is that my son was in my arms and I was wrapped in his. I didn't want to let him go—not then, not ever again. But I did. I stepped aside and gestured toward David.

"Steve, this is your brother, David."

My two sons reached out for one another. What happened next surprised everyone. David wrapped his arms around his brother and sobbed. He was crying so hard, he could hardly speak. He managed to mumble something like, "I've always wondered what happened to you and if you were even still alive. I am so happy to meet you."

I started getting a little teary-eyed then. Every decision we make in life, big or little, ripples out and touches everyone else around us. I was just beginning to find out now how deeply this particular adoption ripple had impacted both of these men.

The rest of the weekend consisted of talking and laughing and eating unbelievably delicious meals that Barb provided—she's a fantastic cook—and talking some more. The only time we separated from each other was for a few hours each night to grab some sleep and then first thing in the morning we were back together and talking again.

What did we talk about?

Everything.

The first thing I remember talking about was the agency. It was at this point in the conversation when I discovered that the letter I had received from the agency forty years ago had been riddled with mistakes. They'd called my baby Brett in the letter. His adoptive parents had named him Steve. *Clerical error, number one.* They said his father was a mechanical engineer and his mother an English teacher. His adoptive father drove a milk truck and his mother was a part-time freelance florist. *Clerical error, number two.* Fast forward to present day. They had searched for me for almost three years and couldn't find me. The investigator did. And last, but certainly not least, was the subject of those two letters I assured Steve I had never received.

For all intents and purposes, there were so many things wrong that it was amazing this meeting was even taking place.

But I firmly believe that everything that has happened to Steve and I both before and since are signs of God's work in our lives. This was His plan and it was happening in His time. We didn't have to worry about clerical errors anymore.

I had already given my son, Steve, a brief synopsis of my life over the phone this past week. Now he was getting a full, no-holds-barred version in even more detail than appears on the pages of this book. I don't know why I did it. Most people would have been more reserved and would have introduced the information in little bites slowly over time, if at all. That's how I would have done it, too, with anybody else. Who wants to air their dirty laundry the first weekend they meet somebody? There are several things I told Steve that no one in my family knows yet today, things that even David was hearing for the first time.

When I met Steve I opened my arms . . . but I also opened my heart . . . completely. I opted to trust him with the most intimate details of my life, with the deepest levels of my pain. I wanted him to know his mother and, I guess, I was trying to fill in forty years in a marathon weekend.

The conversations weren't all dark, deep, and maudlin. There were many funny stories that had all of us laughing and shaking our heads. There were informative stories. *Where did you live at various times in your life? Where did you go on vacations as a child? As an adult?* Surprisingly, as we discussed the geography of our lives, we discovered that we were never far away from one another, almost like we were circling in each other's orbits but not connecting.

One of the questions Steve asked me, I answered without reservation. However, when I asked him a question in return, the answer surprised me and took my breath away:

"Mom, do you mind if I ask if you and my grandmother ever talked about me? I mean after the adoption."

"Your adoption was not openly discussed by anyone in my family," I said. "Not by my siblings and definitely not by my father. But there were three very brief conversations with my mother when the subject of you came up."

I went on to tell him the story of how David had asked about his existence decades ago in the back of our van. As bizarre and unusual as the story was, David, who was sitting with us at the table, confirmed the facts.

Everyone made their various comments on the strangeness of David's questions as a child and then I told Steve about the subsequent telephone call with my mom.

He nodded and looked like he was trying to process the information. "You said there were two other conversations." Steve looked at me and waited for my reply.

"When my grandmother died, my parents flew in for the funeral. One afternoon my mother and I were alone in my apartment. I remember that I was folding towels and putting them in the linen closet. Out of nowhere, and I mean nowhere because we hadn't been having an intimate conversation about anything, my mother turned, pointed her finger at me, and said, 'Maybe what I did wasn't the best thing for you but I know it was the best thing for the baby and if I had it to do over again, I would do the exact same thing.'

"She was visibly upset. On some deep level, I knew that this was my mother's way of apologizing to me. I looked her right in the eye and said, 'You're right, Mom. It wasn't the best thing for me.' Then, I went back to folding clothes and we never discussed you again during that time."

"And the final conversation?" Steve asked.

"The last time we spoke about you I wouldn't really call it a conversation. My mother had Alzheimer's disease. She suffered from it for thirteen years before she died. In the last three years of her life when it didn't matter to her anymore where she lived, Dad moved her out of her Oakland dream house and brought her to Florida so my sister and I could help with her care.

"At this stage of her disease, she didn't seem to recognize anyone by name except my dad. It was sad, really, and bothered my sister the most. After all, my sister had been her favorite. Now, to my mother, she was just a sweet girl. When my sister would try and tell her that she was her daughter, my mother would laugh and say she couldn't be her daughter because she wasn't old enough to have a daughter her age. It really hurt my sister to have lost that relationship with my mother. I had already lost my mother years ago—if I'd ever had her in the first place. But it was still sad to watch what had once been a vibrant, intelligent, well-read woman deteriorate in this manner. Thankfully, my mother recognized my father up to the day she died."

"Anyway, my mother and father moved into a doublewide manufactured home right around the corner from me. I hadn't seen my mother in three, maybe four years, so I walked over to welcome them. My sister and father were already inside the kitchen with my mother when I arrived. When I walked in the back door, my mother took one look at me and said, 'Where's the baby?'

"'What?' I asked.

"'Where's the baby?' she repeated.

"Everybody in the kitchen froze. There was the heaviest silence between my dad, my sister, and me. Finally, I looked at my mother. 'I don't know, Mom. I don't know where the baby is.'

"I took it, at the time, that even in her Alzheimer's state on some deep level, she still thought about you. She still wondered what had happened to you and, even though she denied it, I really believe sometimes she regretted the decision she forced on me. You were her first-born grandchild. She had to wonder about you over the years and that last day in the kitchen, her befuddled mind let us all know that she had."

"I wish my grandparents were still alive," Steve said. "I wish I could have met them. I wonder what they would have said, what they would have felt if they could meet me now."

"Me, too. I particularly wish my father could have lived long enough to meet you."

There was a few seconds lull at the table as we were all lost in our own thoughts when I asked my question.

"Steve," I said. "I've been wondering. The social worker looked for me for almost three years and was not able to find me. Do you know how the private investigator did? Did he find me through my books? I have bios and books on the Internet. Or did he find me through income tax returns or what?"

"He found you through Grandma's obituary," Steve said. "It listed your name and the names of all your siblings. He went from there."

The breath caught in my throat. I couldn't believe what he'd just said. My mother—the woman who had done everything she could to keep my son and me apart—had given him back.

During that first weekend, I had the opportunity to meet Steve's adoptive parents. On Friday night, Steve had only been home about an hour when his adoptive mother, Nancy, called. I heard him say:

"Hi, Mom. Yeah, everything went fine today. Matter of fact, I've had an unbelievable day. You'll never guess who is sitting at my kitchen table. My mother and my brother."

I could hear her screaming through the phone. She sounded so happy and excited.

"Yeah," he said. "I am going to be able to find out about her. I've already found out a lot. Like the fact that she's a liar." Then he went into an imitation of my voice, "Sorry, Steve, but I'm going to be away at a writer's conference in south Florida this weekend." While he was saying this on the phone, he was also standing beside me and gesturing that I had a long Pinocchio nose.

We all burst into laughter. That was the first dose I got of Steve's sense of humor. He sprang it on me several times over the weekend and both David and I not only laughed until we cried then, but laughed over and over again after we were home when we would recant to other family members some of the things he'd said.

His mother, of course, wanted to meet me, too, so she said she would drive over to the house the next day. Saturday afternoon,

Nancy walked in the door. She was carrying a bouquet of pink carnations and dragging a large case behind her. She dropped the case, handed me the flowers, and hugged me tightly.

"Thank you," she whispered in my ear. "Thank you for giving me something that I could never have had any other way."

"Don't thank me," I said. "Thank my mother. It wasn't something I wanted to do."

I wasn't trying to be mean or unappreciative of her words. Truthfully, I was very moved by her kindness and touched by the flowers. But the truth was the truth. Although I was grateful for the excellent job she'd done raising "our" son, I wanted it to be very clear to everyone in that room that I never wanted to give my baby away and had paid a fierce price for that decision.

Nancy had rolled a container on wheels in with her. Within minutes, she was putting one picture after another in front of me as I sat at the kitchen table with the rest of the family. Steve's baby pictures. His first, and subsequent, birthdays. Christmases over the years. Steve on a sled. Steve playing in the snow. Steve riding a toy motorcycle. Every occasion mothers take pictures of their children.

"Here, these are for you," Nancy said, handing me a small packet of pictures. "Every birthday I had a duplicate set made up just in case you ever contacted us. These are the only ones I have with me, but as soon as I get time, I'll sit down and pull out the rest."

I held the pictures of my son, leafing through the pile, watching him mature from infancy through his grammar school days and eventually into his teen years.

I loved seeing the pictures and was grateful to Nancy for sharing them with me. But for the first time, I also felt a wave of sadness sweep over me. As I gazed at the laughing, happy face of my son, as I flipped through all the pictures of his life, I realized that I had missed it all.

Late Saturday afternoon, Steve, Barb, and I drove to the hospital to visit Steve's adoptive father, who was going to need a skin graft on his leg due to diabetic complications. The visit was short, but accomplished what it had intended. Steve's dad and I got to meet and exchange pleasantries.

As we were leaving the hospital, I started thinking about the past week.

Between our telephone conversations and this weekend visit, I had told Steve every single detail of my life both good and bad. I filled up with tears and turned to face him in the corridor leading to the parking lot.

"Steve, can I ask you a question?"

He stopped, glanced at Barb and then back at me. "Sure. What?"

"Now that you've met me. Now that I've told you everything there is to tell about me. Are you sorry you searched?"

I held my breath while I waited for his response. He took a couple of steps toward me, looked at me, and said, "No, Ma." He stared right into my eyes. "No. Never."

I hadn't been wrong to trust him. We had a bond between us, a bond that over time was going to do nothing but get stronger.

It was hard to say good-bye that weekend. I'd just been reunited with my son and I couldn't get enough of him. I loved listening to the deep, rich tones of his voice. I enjoyed listening to him tell me stories that he wanted me to know about his life. I loved watching him clown around and tease me. I particularly loved watching him interact with his family, knowing now that I was a part of that family.

What made it easier to leave was the knowledge that it wouldn't be long until we were together again. It was the middle of April. Steven, my oldest grandson, would be graduating from high school the end of May. I was barely out of the driveway before my mind began scheming about ways to come back for it.

The telephone calls from Steve came right on the dot at seven o'clock every night. During one of those calls, the subject of Steven's graduation came up and I tentatively broached the subject about coming for it. The Orlandi family was thrilled I would be willing to come back that soon. When they found out that David and his wife, Esther, wanted to fly out for that weekend, too, we started making definite plans.

Since I had already told Steve that his Uncle Michael and family were coming to Florida for a vacation, another road trip came to fruition. Steve suggested he drive down the weekend after Mother's Day, visit with me, see my home, meet some of my friends, and then drive into Orlando to meet both uncles, their families, and his other brother, Dan, and his family.

It sounded wonderful to me.

To make it even better, Steve and Barb decided to drive me back with them. I'd stay the week. I'd be there for the graduation and I'd be there to greet Dave and Esther when they flew in. Then, Steve could take me to the airport Sunday night and I could fly home.

Nine days with my son and his family. Count me in!

◦ ❃ ◦

The weekend that Steve and Barb arrived was everything and more than I'd hoped it would be. They toured my home and the amenities of my retirement community. They stayed in a condo on the beach—the Outrigger Beach Club to be exact—the time-share that Bill and I had sold units for when we lived in Michigan when we'd first met.

Now Bill was gone, but I was here at the Outrigger looking out over the ocean with my long-lost son by my side.

God's plans for our lives sometimes crack me up with their irony.

Oh, and by the way, did I remember to tell you that Barb found a bright shiny penny in the parking lot?

◦ ⁂ ◦

Steve and Barb were looking forward to the trip into Orlando to meet the rest of the family. I was a little nervous. I knew my siblings and their families would be warm and gracious when they met him. I was more concerned about how this meeting would affect my son, Dan. I knew he was genuinely happy for me that Steve had found me and wanted to develop a relationship with me. But the whole idea had slapped him upside the head without warning and I wasn't so sure he'd had sufficient time to come to grips with it all. I can still remember him shaking his head and saying, "I can't believe I've gone from being the oldest to suddenly being someone's kid brother."

When we pulled up to my brother's condominium complex, half of my family was already upstairs in the condo. My grandchildren were in the pool and, Dan, his wife Claudia, and my brother, Tom, were sitting at a table nearby keeping an eye on the kids. When they saw us arrive, Tom and Dan walked over to the gate to greet us. Claudia stayed behind with the kids.

Steve shook Tom's hand. When Steve approached Dan, he leaned toward him. I was surprised to see Dan man-hug him back. You know, the kind of hug where it is really more grasping each other's arms with both hands and lasts about three seconds, but is definitely more intimate and inviting than a plain handshake.

Before any conversations could start, Tom efficiently herded us toward the condo, telling us that my other brother, Michael, and his family and my niece, and all the cousins were already waiting for us upstairs. Dan turned and joined Claudia back at the pool.

More than a dozen family members were upstairs. After introductions, Steve and Barb sat on the sofa and Steve told his version of his search and his reaction to the first telephone call with his mother. It was a moving rendition, caused a chuckle here and there and brought a tear to more than one eye in the room.

I sat on the sidelines with a wide grin on my face and watched. I was so proud of my son. He'd watched this exact moment happen on television for someone else years ago, and now it was happening to him. He'd walked into a room full of strangers and found his family waiting and happy to meet him.

About that time, Tom came into the condo and told Steve and Barb that Dan wanted to know if he would come down to the pool area.

All three of us stood to go and Tom flagged me back down. "Not you, Diane."

"What? Why not?" I asked.

"Because Dan wants to talk to Steve without you there."

Steve saw the worried expression on my face and said, "Don't worry, Ma. I'm a big boy. I can take care of myself. Sit down and visit with the rest of your family. Barb and I shouldn't be too long." They grabbed some cold sodas for everyone at the pool. At the door, Steve stopped and looked back at me. "Ma, I don't want to look up at the window and see you like Garfield pressed against the glass. Relax. Enjoy your visit. Everything's going to be fine."

I sat back down, but I didn't relax. I couldn't imagine why Dan would be adamant that I not go downstairs. None of it made sense. My family members tried to distract me and I played along with them, but it wasn't working. I could barely keep my eyes off my watch.

When more than an hour passed and no one had come back from the pool, I had had enough. I told Tom I was going downstairs to see what was going on. When I got to the pool, I was surprised and pleased with what I saw. My grandkids were still playing in the pool. Steve, Barb, Claudia, and Dan were sitting at a table nearby. They were laughing and talking to each other like old friends.

Later, of course, I questioned Dan as to why he did things the way he did. He told me it would have felt awkward for him to try and hold a conversation with Steve upstairs with half of our family watching and clinging on their every word. He'd asked me to stay away because he wanted to form his own opinion of Steve, and it would be easier for him to do it if he wasn't worried about me or my feelings.

All in all, both my sons were right. It was the perfect way for the two brothers to connect and I had nothing to worry about. And connect they did.

Steve

After I received the tour of my mom's house and neighborhood, and after staying at the timeshare resort that was instrumental in bringing my mom to Florida, I was really looking forward to going down to Orlando to meet some more of my family.

I was able to meet two uncles, two aunts, tons of cousins, my other brother, my sister-in-law, and my nephews for the first time.

I think the most surprising thing about the whole weekend was that I felt completely comfortable. I did not feel overwhelmed in that big group setting even though I am a solitary person. I felt completely at ease. I looked around the room and my mind kept saying to me *That's your uncle, That's your aunt, That's your other uncle, That's your brother, Those are your cousins.* This time I welcomed that voice that had nagged me on and off since the age of six. I knew for the first time in my life that I wasn't pretending anymore.

The relationships weren't there yet and were just beginning, but just the fact that I didn't have to pretend anymore was a relief. Nobody in that room could say I didn't belong here. These people were my real, biological family and that bond was the first taste of big family that I got.

I enjoyed that visit immensely and I still look forward to someday meeting the rest of them. I've connected with most of them online. Slowly, I'm sure I'll meet them at some point in the years to come as my "clan" gathers for family occasions.

The situation could have been strange for me because I didn't know these people. I knew my adoptive family, my adoptive parents, grandparents, aunts, uncles, cousins, and I loved them, but there was always that "pretend" cloud hovering above it.

But the situation wasn't strange. In fact, it was the complete opposite of strange. I didn't know them, but I felt like I loved them and I now knew that I belonged to that group. So it was really crazy.

If I divided the room into two sides, I'd have the adoptive parents whom I know and love and know everything about, but they're not really my blood relatives, and then on the other side are the biological family that I'm blood-related to but I don't know.

It messed with my mind. It felt just as strange and surreal as the day I knew I was going to talk to my mother for the first time and get all my answers at seven o'clock that night.

It takes an adjustment period. Who knows how long that adjustment period is? I'm still going through it.

Chapter

14

Diane

The Sunday before we drove home, Steve and Barb accompanied me to my church. I was appreciative that they did because Steve doesn't have any strong religious convictions, doesn't attend church, and it was obvious he did it to please me. He told me later that he was surprised but that he had really enjoyed the sermon and meeting with my friends.

I wasn't surprised. Number one, the people at Crossroads Calvary Chapel are warm and welcoming. Number two, God had His hands all over this entire reunion. It shouldn't have surprised Steve at all that he had heard a little of God's voice in that Sunday sermon.

Steve drove home. Barb sat beside him in the passenger seat and I was in the back. On the way home, I broached a subject I had been concerned about.

"Steve, can I ask you something? Did you find it difficult to forgive me?"

My eyes caught and held with his in the rearview mirror. He looked puzzled. "Forgive you for what?"

"Giving you away."

"There's nothing to forgive, Mom. You've told me the whole story and, truthfully, you had no choice. The only anger I feel is maybe a little bit of anger toward all the family members who hurt you in your life. This life is tough. We should be able to trust the people closest to us. You were hurt by people who never should have hurt you. That makes me mad.

"But I'm not mad at you. I understand what happened. Besides, I had a good childhood. I was a happy kid. I have nothing to be angry with you about."

Just about that time, nature called and I asked Steve to stop at a rest area. He pulled into a fast food establishment and dropped Barb and I at the door, telling us he'd wait in the car.

I headed for the bathroom. Barb went to the counter and placed an order. When I came out of the bathroom, I joined her at the counter. She asked if I wanted anything and I told her no. Since she was still waiting for her order, I told her that I was going to go outside and wait in the car with Steve.

I walked out to the parking lot, glanced at the cars, and didn't see Steve. Thinking I probably went out the wrong door, I walked back inside, crossed the building, and went out the other door to that parking lot.

No Steve.

So I went back inside to the counter to ask Barb if she knew where he was.

No Barb.

I went back outside both doors twice more thinking maybe I had mistaken what car he was driving.

Still no sign of either one of them.

I had just sat down at a table and was trying to decide what I should do next when I saw Steve pull into the parking lot like a Nascar driver. He jumped out of the car and greeted me as I walked toward him.

"I'm sorry, Ma." He was laughing his head off. "I went to get gas. When I texted Barb and told her to tell you, she texted back that she was in the restroom and that you had already gone out to the parking lot." He tried hard to control his laughter but couldn't and kept cracking up.

"I can only imagine what you must have been thinking when both Barb and I disappeared," he said. "Particularly since we'd just had that conversation about whether I was angry with you. I guess dumping you in a fast food joint in another state and taking off could qualify as being angry."

Steve laughed about the whole thing. He laughed for days and days to come every time it crossed his mind.

Truthfully, I did too.

Steve

My son, Steven's, graduation was probably the first time I actually got visibly emotional about anything in quite a while. Meeting my mother and brother had been unbelievable enough and had moved me deeply even if I didn't let myself show it. But Steven's graduation. That put me over the top. I was such a proud father. I am extremely proud of both my sons, but this particular day my focus was on Steven. This was a significant milestone in his life and in mine and I couldn't keep my emotions from showing.

When we were all sitting in the bleachers, ironically at the college that Steven was going to be attending, I kind of took a mental step back. I watched and clapped as he walked on stage and accepted his diploma and my eyes never left him as he walked back down to his seat. I heard my adoptive mother whistling and other family members shouting and cheering and calling Steven's name.

And then it hit me.

I was sitting at my first-born son's graduation, one of the most significant moments of our family lives, and I was with my adoptive parents, my wife, my step-daughter, my son, Kevin, and miraculously with my mother, my brother, and his wife.

It hit me hard that there were three people there to see my son graduate who, just a little more than a month before, I hadn't even known existed. I couldn't have ever imagined this could be possible.

As most of the days after I'd met my mother for the first time, this one was dreamlike. It wasn't just that my son was graduating, which was emotional enough for me as it was, but the fact that my mother and my brother were there to see it affected me strongly. That was the second most terrific weekend in my life.

Diane

The hustle and bustle of everyone preparing for the graduation felt as normal, hectic, and fun as any other gathering I had ever had with my siblings and children. But this one was different. This was a family that, six weeks ago, I hadn't had a clue even existed.

Yet, here we were.

Sharing the bathrooms for last minute makeup and clothing adjustments. Milling in the kitchen trying to snitch a bite from some of the goodies Barbara had prepared for the open house following the ceremony. Yelling and calling out for everyone to hurry up so we could take family pictures in the front yard.

I heard my son, David, laughing in the next room, probably at some sarcastic remark Steve had made.

I watched Barbara mumbling a checklist under her breath so she wouldn't forget anything for the party while simultaneously making sure Steven was dressed to the nines and wearing his honors medal.

I teased Kevin, pet the dogs Beau and Bella, followed Barb around asking if she needed my help, and spent some time talking with Esther.

It was a relaxing, fun, exciting time and I couldn't believe how happy I was or how much at home I felt with this family. But then . . . I should have felt that way. It was my family—a family of strangers I was quickly coming to love.

We drove in a caravan to the college and sat in a slow-moving traffic pattern until we were directed to our spot in the parking lot. Steve jumped out as soon as we parked and hurried ahead to meet up with his adoptive parents. His father was in a wheelchair because of the skin graft on his leg. Steve wanted to help his mother make sure she could manage getting him from the car into the auditorium. The rest of us walked in one large, talking, laughing group until we found our way inside.

Because of the wheelchair, Steve's adoptive parents weren't able to sit with the rest of us in the bleachers. But Steve sat as close to them as possible and found us seats together only four rows below.

I had not been feeling well for the last couple of months and was a bit uncomfortable with our seats. I was worried that if I needed to use a restroom, I would be disrupting everyone by trying to climb over them to get out of the row. I told Barb that I was going to go around to the other side and sit on the end of the row so I'd be able to get up and leave if I needed to without disturbing anyone.

As I climbed the stairs to make my way around to the other set of steps leading to the far side of our row, I spotted Nancy and Joe, Steve's parents.

"Do you mind if I sit with you?" I asked.

"Not at all. Please, have a seat," Nancy replied.

Steve grinned and shook his head when he saw all three of his parents sitting together.

Yeah, this was an unusual day for all of us.

While we were waiting for the ceremony to begin, Nancy started talking to me. She told me different stories about Steve as a small boy. Different things he liked and things he didn't. She talked about teaching Steve how to throw a baseball and how much he had loved baseball as a child. She told me about standing in the hospital, seeing her grandson, Steven, in his bassinet. She said she had been there, right by Steven's side, for every birthday and important day of his life. She stated how unbelievable it was to her that the years had passed so quickly and she was now sitting at his graduation.

Listening to the things Nancy said caused me the same pain I experienced looking at the pictures. I had missed out on both my son's life and my grandchildren's. I hadn't raised my child, she had. She was the one who had rocked him to sleep at night, who had heard his first word, who had watched him take his first step.

Nancy had sent him off on his first day of school. Had built snowmen in the yard with him. And sent him sailing down a hill on a sled. These were all memories that belonged to the woman beside me. They weren't mine to claim.

Nancy was Steve's mother.

I don't know if it makes sense to anyone other than me, but the truth of the matter was that I was equally grateful and resentful. She had done for my son what I hadn't been able to do for him on my own. She had done a wonderful job. Steve constantly told me what a happy childhood he had. And he'd grown up to be a wonderful man. I would owe Nancy my undying gratitude for the rest of my life.

But Nancy had also had all those moments, all those wonderful, cherished moments that I had forever lost.

It also saddened me that I had missed out on both my grandsons' lives. I'd seen pictures of them as toddlers and as young boys. I saw them playing at the shore and clowning around at family gatherings. But I had missed being able to develop that unique relationship between grandparent and grandchild.

Now I was sitting at my first grandson's graduation. It was an awesome, exciting, happy time.

But I also had a very heavy heart.

I smiled and nodded and said very little to Nancy when she was telling me those stories. I wondered why she had. She must have known how difficult it would be for me to sit there and listen to her reminisce over events and activities that I would have given almost anything to have lived through myself.

I hate to admit it, but I was jealous. Green-eyed envy raced through every pore of my body. I truly believed, at that moment, that she was purposely telling me those stories to mark her territory, to remind me that she was the mother to my son and she was the grandmother to my grandsons.

Jealousy is an evil thing. It sees deception and pride and manipulation where none exists. I am ashamed that I harbored those feelings. It took me a very long time to understand that she had done nothing wrong and that I was the one who had character flaws that needed work.

Nancy bragged about her son and grandson that day because she was a proud mother and a proud grandmother. She would have bragged to anyone and everyone she could. She was happy and excited and cheering Steven on. She let out a whistle that would have stopped a train when she saw him step up on the platform to accept his diploma.

Even though I thought she was a threat to me, I was wrong. Nancy already knew what it took me much longer to figure out: Steve's heart was big enough for both of us. We both have equal but different roles to play in his life. He needs us both. He loves us both and he always will.

Nancy knew from the first second I showed up on Steve's doorstep that I was going to be a permanent fixture in their family. So she accepted it and welcomed me with open arms. She was secure enough in her relationship with Steve that I posed no threat to her and she was genuinely grateful that because of me, whether willingly or not, I had provided her with the opportunity to raise and love a child.

I learned a lot from Nancy. I just wish it hadn't taken me so long.

❦

When I hugged my son, Steve, good-bye at the airport the night after the graduation, I thought my heart was going to break. The more I got to know him, the more I wanted to be with him. The more time I spent with his family, the harder it was for me to leave.

We had lost so much time.

Forty years.

How was I going to live with frequent telephone calls and every-other-month visits?

Instead of being grateful for what I had, my human nature came to the forefront and I wanted more.

I hoped and prayed that no matter how painful the good-byes were, I never would stop wanting to be with my son. I found out fast enough that I didn't have anything to worry about. I'd wanted to be with my son for more than forty years. Those feelings certainly weren't going to stop now.

Chapter

15

Diane

One of the inevitable challenges Steve and I had to face—and are still facing—is how to build a healthy, long-lasting relationship when, biological mother and son or not, you are still strangers with decades of living separate lives between you.

But one of the most beautiful, awesome blessings that God gave Steve and I was an instant bond and an almost overwhelming love for each other. We couldn't explain it to others because we couldn't explain it to ourselves.

I only know from that very first telephone conversation on April 10 when I heard my son's voice say "Hello, Mom" that my heart burst wide open with love and happiness and joy. This was my lost baby, the one I was certain I would never see again this side of heaven, speaking to me. Wanting to meet me. Wanting to build a relationship with me. Wanting to love me. God had given me such an awesome gift.

In the first few months of our relationship, we both did everything in our power to connect, to savor every second together, whether it was morning texts on our cell phones, lengthy phone conversations every night, or visiting each other every opportunity we could. It was less than forty-five days into our relationship when my son approached me with news.

He had decided that due to his father's failing health, he wanted to be more of a help to his adoptive parents as they aged. He planned on selling his house and buying a larger house, one with a comfortable ground floor apartment for his parents so he could be there when they needed him. What surprised me is what came next.

One evening, during the week I was visiting so I could attend my grandson's graduation, Steve and I were sitting on the porch, which had become our favorite place to disappear after dinner. He was swinging on his swing. I was sitting in the wicker chair beside him.

"Mom, I'd like to talk to you about something."

I smiled and waited to hear what he had to say. He'd already told me on the phone the week before that he planned on selling his home and moving his parents closer.

"Since I'm going to the trouble and expense of buying a larger house," he said, "I want you to know that Barb and I and the kids took a family vote and we'd like to invite you to move in with us."

I couldn't believe what I was hearing. Move in with them? I was surprised and thrilled and honored. "Are you sure?"

"Of course I'm sure," Steve said. "I've talked with the family and they agreed. There wasn't even one negative vote or remark."

He grinned at me. "If I can do this for my adoptive parents, then how can I *not* find a place in my home for my mother?"

I was deeply moved by his sincerity and by the revelation that his feelings for me were as strong as mine for him. Obviously, in hindsight, neither one of us was thinking straight. We'd been back in one another's lives only forty-five days and we were still flying high with happiness and excitement.

When he saw my hesitancy and uncertainty, he continued. "We've lost too much time, Ma. You and I don't know how much time we have left together. Ten years? Fifteen? Less?

"I only know that I don't want to waste a day of it. I don't want to settle for telephone calls at night and weekend visits every other month. I want to see you every day . . . in my home . . . sitting at my dinner table . . . interacting with my family. We've waited years for this, Ma. It's our turn now. We *both* deserve this."

Even though I make my living as an author, I am unable to find the words to express what an impact my son's decision had on me. I can only tell you I was touched beyond measure and that I didn't know a human heart could truly feel such absolute joy.

Whether I moved into his home wasn't as important to me as the knowledge that he wanted me to, that his family wanted me, as well. Steve, Barb, my wonderful grandchildren, and Steve's adoptive parents had already blessed me with more than I ever expected or felt I deserved. They had already opened their family and their hearts to include me. Now Steve wanted to make me a permanent daily fixture in his home. My gratitude for their love and acceptance was endless.

When Steve prepared to put his house up for sale and we told everyone our plans, family and friends on both sides of the fence had understandable reservations.

Steve had someone close to him respectfully ask, "You're moving in all *three* parents? Are you sure you want to do this?"

He replied, "Yes. My parents need me and I need my mother."

On my side of the fence, one of my brothers, who always had my best interest at heart, asked, "Aren't you moving too fast?

It's great your son found you. I'm happy for you. I really am. But you are still strangers to one another. You should be taking baby steps. Slow things down. What's the hurry?"

When Steve and I discussed their well-intentioned hesitations, he said, "They don't understand, Mom. Nobody can understand this except us. But don't worry. In time, they will. It's going to take time to sell our homes and it's going to take even more time to find the right house, one that will satisfy everyone's needs. By then everyone will be able to tell that our relationship is solid and lasting or it isn't."

My son never spoke truer words.

Time reveals everything.

Steve and I discovered over time that no relationship can sustain that happy, honeymoon-period high that people experience when love is new and fresh and exciting. Whether it is a mother with her brand new baby, a teen falling in love for the first time, newlyweds adjusting to married life—or a mother and son who had been separated for more than forty years and were now together again.

As I've said before, we all know there are no such things as perfect people. This applies to Steve and me, as well.

When the thrill and excitement of reuniting wore off and day-to-day living came into play, it was another major adjustment for both of us.

For the rest of the world, relationships start out slowly. You meet one another, start to like one another, grow to know one another, and then over time come to love one another.

Steve and I had to go through the process backwards. We felt a strong instant bond and love for one another from the very beginning. Now we had to find out whether we *liked* one another. We had to learn all about each other. Then we had to hope and pray that the feelings we had in the very beginning were not only real, but that they were strong enough to survive the backward journey.

Steve never lost confidence. He'd always say, "Ma, don't worry about what anybody else says. Our relationship might take some dings and scratches, maybe even a little dent here and there as we get to know one another, but that's okay. Because the core of this relationship is solid. The core is built on love. You are my mother. I am your son. Nothing is ever going to change that."

Steve was so certain that we could withstand anything that came our way that he showed me a picture of the two of us together. "Mom, remember that bible verse from Ruth that you sent to me? I'm going to mount this picture on a plaque and have the verse engraved beneath it."

The Bible verse was Ruth, Chapter 1, Verse 17:

"May the Lord do terrible things to me if I allow anything but death to separate us."

Over time, my son's belief that our relationship could last was tested. The early hurdles were subtle, but slowly escalated and became more difficult. From the very first day, we discovered the surface things about each other and it was fun. Physically, Steve had the same shaped hands and feet as me. He had the same color eyes and the same round face.

We discovered several things we shared in common. We both liked the color blue. We preferred our meat cooked well done. We loved our family more than anything on Earth. We loved dogs and couldn't tolerate cats. We liked swimming pools and the beaches in Florida, and we both had a creative side geared for writing.

I also discovered he could clean a house better than anyone I've ever met. Me—not so much. He has a wicked sense of humor and the ability to make you laugh even when you don't want to. Me—not so much. He doesn't watch much television and isn't into movies. Me—I'm a movieholic and TIVO every show on television if I think there's even a remote possibility I might miss something. He is an extremely hard-working, responsible person. Me? I'm working on it.

But then came the harder part of getting to know each other. The part that involved questions of character, habits, and expectations. The part that required patience and dedication and digging beneath the surface if we truly wanted more than a simple, superficial relationship. We both had to decide if we were willing to risk disappointment, if we were willing to delve deeper no matter where the road took us.

After a lifetime of disappointments and heartache, I believed that when it came to dealing with people, the wise thing to do was to protect your heart, expect nothing from them, and be pleasantly surprised if you got anything in return. I didn't believe much in people's ability to be loyal or honest and for years I had found it very difficult to trust.

But here I was—opening my heart without reservation, trusting, believing, loving—confident that this time it was going to be all right.

When my son started his search, he had only wanted one thing: answers. I don't think he ever imagined that the last thing he wanted—a relationship with a stranger, a second mother, a complication in his otherwise ordinary, happy life—just might be the one thing that he really needed.

So as we slowly climbed down from the euphoric high of that mountain top and planted our feet firmly on solid ground, we learned more about each other, and they weren't always easy lessons to learn.

How do we cope with disappointments? How do we handle having opposite opinions on important matters such as religion, politics, ethics? Are we cut from the same moral cloth in regard to honesty, integrity, and keeping our word?

What about arguments? How do we react the first time one of us snaps at the other? How do we handle true anger? Are we spiteful people? Do we belittle and call names or do we calm down and talk things out? Do we hold grudges or do we have the ability to forgive and move on?

Everyone needs to discover these things about the people they want to form permanent relationships with if the relationship is to last and grow. But usually they have the luxury of taking their time, like my brother said—baby steps.

But when you've lost forty years, when one of you has more time behind than ahead, time becomes critical.

Steve and I already thought we had the love and the bond. But did we?

Learning about each other's character was similar to taking a very complex college course in the accelerated summer program. The material to be learned was the same as through the more relaxed fall/spring semesters, but the pressure and the time restraints to learn it during a brief summer course comes at you at breakneck speed.

So we experienced our first skirmishes, our first disappointments in each other, our first hurts. We didn't have a family history between us to draw upon to help us through it, either—I didn't raise this child so I didn't recognize his hot buttons, his temperament, his personality quirks. He didn't live with me for forty years, either. He hadn't built forty years of trust. He didn't know what he could and couldn't say or do without hurting my feelings so he often held back saying things he should have said and it led to frustration and eventually hurt and anger.

A tiny example of how a little thing blew up into a bigger one:

My son likes to start his day at 5:30 a.m. He likes the quiet and solitude of his house before the rest of his family gets up. He is a private person and, although equally sociable and people-oriented, I believe he is able to be that fun, loving, people-person by stoking up on his quiet, personal time when he needs it.

I was staying with him for a week. I am not a morning person. I even wear a sleep mask to bed so the sun doesn't wake me when it filters through the window.

My son had to work during my visit, resulting in only having a few hours in the evening for us to spend together. So I got the brilliant idea to get up every morning and keep him company before he left for work.

He never told me he is a private person. He never told me how important it is to him to have his alone time for fear of hurting my feelings. I never told him that I couldn't stand getting up at the crack of dawn and plastering a smile on my face when I don't normally open an eye until nine. So we suffered, and frustrations grew, and it bled from one visit over to the next.

Such a little incident. One of many inconsequential things that could have been avoided if we had just felt comfortable enough with each other to speak our minds. Those unspoken frustrations led to more disappointments and more hurt feelings as other problems surfaced and our communication skills faltered and our ability to speak honestly with each other didn't seem to exist.

Forty years makes a difference. Those years were lived by both of us with other people in other places. They were gone and there was nothing we could do to get them back. We both discovered the hard truth: it isn't easy to love a stranger.

These skirmishes and disappointments were just the beginning. The biggest hurdle was yet to come.

In time, the offer to move into Steve's house was rescinded. When he really had time to sit down and think things through—which he admits he should have done before he invited me to move in, but he had acted with his heart and not his head—he realized that privacy would be a major issue. His youngest child, Kevin, was just two years away from graduating from high school and heading to college.

Two years.

For the very first time since the day Steve had married Barb, it would be just the two of them. They'd never had a honeymoon. They'd never taken a vacation that didn't entail taking children with them. They'd done things backwards, started their relationship with three children and built from there. They never had that special one-on-one time in the very beginning of their marriage before children arrive that almost every other marriage has the opportunity to experience.

Steve and Barbara were about to enter a new phase of their relationship. A house without children. A life without family responsibilities.

Oh, wait a minute!

Not with Steve's original mother living in the house and his adoptive parents living in an in-law apartment below.

So there were many discussions. Some hurt feelings. Some disappointments.

Steve's adoptive parents had no problems with his change of plans. They had a forty-one year history with him. They loved him and knew he loved them. They knew what kind of man he was. They were secure in the knowledge that whatever the new plan would be, Steve would be there for them, helping them when needed, loving them for the rest of their lives. This was their son, a good man, a reliable man, and they knew without doubt that they were in good hands.

Me—not so much.

When I took my house back off the market and faced the reality that I wouldn't be moving into Steve's house, it honestly devastated me. Like I said before, it never mattered to me whether I moved into Steve's house. I had a house already that I had lived in for fourteen years. I am independent and quite capable of earning my own living. I've done it all my life. What mattered was the fact that he had *wanted* me to live with him. Now he didn't.

Because of all the rejection and betrayals I had faced throughout my life, I saw this as just one more rejection—and this time from the very last person I wanted to be rejected by. I didn't allow myself to listen to his plans or even try to understand the logic of his reasoning. I took it very personally. Steve didn't want me. In my mind, that translated to the idea that he didn't love me. He was pulling away and rejecting me just like my mother, my husband, and my sister had done.

It took forever for Steve to pound it into my head that this decision had nothing to do with me. He didn't want *anyone* to move into his house after the children left.

No one.

For privacy purposes.

He wasn't rejecting me. He didn't love me one iota less. He would always be there for me. He even strongly encouraged me to sell my house and move closer so we could see each other more frequently and he would be available for whatever help I should need.

Around this same time, I had met two people at my church who had also had adoption reunion experiences. One of them had been found by her birth father. She didn't want anything to do with him. She told him he'd given up his right to fatherhood when he walked away. She even took out a restraining order against him. The second woman I met had had a reunion with her daughter that lasted several years when she received a letter stating, "You are really a nice woman but I have to end this relationship.

I have a mother and there just isn't any place in my life for you."
This woman warned me to tread carefully and guard my heart,
that the pain of losing her daughter twice was devastating.

Now Steve was rescinding his offer. How could I believe it
wasn't personal? How could I possibly believe this relationship
would last?

I love you and this decision was not personal.

That became Steve's new mantra and the poor guy had to
repeat it almost every time he spoke to me on the phone for
weeks, truthfully many, many months, before I finally understood he was telling me the truth.

I wasn't being rejected or thrown away. It was old wounds,
old fears that had crept back into my psyche. And they came
back with a vengeance.

At the same time Steve rescinded his offer, I was working on
the manuscript for this book. This story took me emotionally to
places I had buried deep within for almost a lifetime. It made
me relive incidents I didn't want to have to ever think about
again, to feel pain I had never allowed myself to process.

It also caused a deep divide within my family. Some siblings
were supportive; others became angry and, eventually, disowned
me. They were embarrassed and didn't want their family's "dirty
laundry" aired for public viewing. They felt what had gone on
in our home was private and should be kept that way.

Also at this time, my health was on a decline. I had been to
several doctors, had every test conceived by man, and am still
without a diagnosis. Thankfully, today the doctors have me on a
medical regimen that has controlled the symptoms, returned the
quality of my life, and made living more pleasurable. But at this
particular time, when I felt the world was collapsing around my
head, I was also sick and housebound and miserable.

And, of course, it never rains, but it pours.

My roommate moved out, taking a sizeable part of my monthly income along. One of the part-time jobs I had folded. I suffered writer's block and couldn't come up with even one new story idea or plot. All of it resulted in my finances taking a major hit and my stress level creeping to meltdown stage.

I became weepy and clingy and bombarded Steve on every telephone call with tears and pity-me stories. At first he was sympathetic, but as time went on, the harder I clung, the more Steve pulled away. He became distant. But he still called like clockwork. He didn't give up and he didn't leave.

Eventually the old 2007 thoughts of walking into the ocean swept over me. I was certain I was unlovable, unworthy, and unwanted. Hadn't life already proven that to me? I could hear all the years of criticism from my mother racing through my mind. I relived all the pain and loss that resulted from the pregnancy and adoption. I relived the pain of my sister's betrayal and my divorce. My husband, Bill, was dead and I was lonely. My other sons had families of their own and lived far from me so I convinced myself I wasn't needed. And I was certain my relationship with Steve couldn't last.

Poor Steve had to listen to all this garbage. He had just found his mother, someone he had wondered about for years, and she was talking about ending her life. He grew angrier. He couldn't understand why he wasn't enough to live for, why my other sons and all my grandchildren weren't enough to make me happy?

How could he be expected to understand when I didn't understand either?

I wasn't doing this on purpose. I just hadn't been mentally or emotionally equipped to handle *everything* that was coming at me all at once. I had lived a life of betrayal and rejection and emotional abuse. I had never gone for help to learn how to cope with the problems and resulting pain.

My severe depression damaged our relationship.

But it didn't end it.

Steve kept asking me to go back to church. He kept telling me I was a different person, a happier person, when I was on daily speaking terms with God.

I have no idea why I temporarily stepped away from my faith. When I should have found strength in my beliefs, I acted like I had no belief at all.

I am deeply ashamed of what I put Steve through and humiliated to have to admit that I did.

But this memoir is the truth about our reunion and it wouldn't be the complete, open, honest story if I left it out to save myself embarrassment.

Eventually I got professional help and it was the best thing I ever did. It helped me process the pain I was feeling and finally close the door on the past. It was like taking off a heavy, sodden winter coat and stepping out into the light. I have faced my demons. My past does not define me anymore.

I returned to church and, more importantly, I returned to God and found Him loving and forgiving and right there waiting for me. I know I may experience sadness for one reason or the other in the future, but I also believe from the bottom of my heart that I will never fall into one of those suicidal, depressive holes again. Because I know that whatever difficult situations life dishes my way, my Lord is right beside me giving me the strength, the inner peace, and the support I'll need.

For the very first time, I can look at myself in the mirror and not feel shame and guilt looking back. I no longer have to wear a public mask. I have always believed no one could like me if they knew the real me. Now, I not only respect myself, but I am proud of my accomplishments and truly like myself.

When Steve opened that door, he wasn't the only thing that came through. But I thank God he did because I can truthfully say the past has no more hold on me and I am free!

Steve, although going through all his own emotions regarding the reunion, showed me infinite patience, love, commitment, and he waited. He more than waited. He continued to call. He constantly reassured me. He put up with his emotional, needy mamma until she could look him in the eye and trust that he wasn't going anywhere. Not now. Not ever.

And, finally, one day I got myself together.

The helium joy faded and day-to-day life took over. I discovered that I wasn't giddy and silly and almost obsessed anymore with this stranger that had re-entered my life—because now he wasn't a stranger.

I was getting to know him and as I learned more about him, I grew to love him more and more each day. I was becoming comfortable with him and no longer walking on eggshells or bending over backward trying to please him. I was just being me, being Mom.

I found I could talk to him about anything and everything. I could nag him like mothers sometimes do. I could get angry with him every once in a while and he didn't go running for the hills when I did. He'd wait for me to calm down and then we'd talk out the problem.

I was happy again, deep in my heart and in my soul happy.

We never truly understand God's timing or His plan for our lives. But if I dare to take a guess, I'd say He set the pieces in motion that would help me heal old wounds and find happiness and peace in the remaining days of my life.

God knows where I've been, how I have suffered from the consequences of poor choices that I've made. He knows the pain I've endured from the betrayals and rejections from people I should have been able to trust.

And He knows that I finally and completely turned my life and heart over to Him.

He has turned my life completely around, from ashes built beauty and joy. What a wonderful blessing and plan He has put in place for me now.

For anyone reading these words who might be contemplating a reunion, both Steve and I agree, the most important thing to take from this memoir is to go *slowly!* As my brother said, take baby steps, don't make any permanent decisions or take any leaps until you truly get to know each other.

All reunions are intense, emotional, and complicated. It is the past colliding with the present and being faced with an uncertain future. It is joy and pain and hope and disappointment. But it can *become* a relationship founded on love and blessed with commitment and happiness. By the time people read this book, two years will have passed since that first life-changing telephone call.

Our relationship is no longer comprised of unrealistic expectations and helium-joy giddiness.

It is so much better.

It is normal and quiet and uneventful. It is comfortable and dependable. It is fun and sometimes surprising and, most importantly, filled with love.

I remember one particular day on Sanibel Island in Florida. Every year for the past twenty years, Steve and Barb took their kids and vacationed with Barb's family on the island. They'd all rent condos near one another and spend a couple of weeks reconnecting and playing and relaxing as a family.

Our first year back together, Steve invited me to join them.

I got to meet Barb's family and their friends. At one point we were twenty-eight people trying to get reservations at a local restaurant for dinner together. It was a time of fun and laughter, talking, fishing, partying, looking for shells, playing board games and card games and just being together as a family enjoying each other's company and loving each other.

I was deeply touched that Steve wanted me included in something so personal and important to him and his family.

Midweek my daughter-in-law, Barb, was tanning on the beach. My grandson, Kevin, was with his cousins clowning around back at the pool. Steve and his son, Steven, were standing in waist-high water in the gulf and taking turns diving and digging for shells.

I was floating in the gulf about a dozen feet away from them.

My son, being an analytical person, came to know me, my personality and my idiosyncrasies, much faster than I expected. I still smile when I think about the resulting conversation.

"Ma, what are you thinking about?" he yelled over to me.

"What?" I had been deep in thought, but I had no clue how he knew. To anyone else I would have just looked like I was floating away without a care in the world.

"You've got your index finger against your lips," Steve said. "You always do that when you're thinking. So what are you thinking about?"

He was right. My index finger was resting against my lips. I laughed and moved it. Even *I* didn't realize I did that when lost in thought. My son doesn't miss much.

"Do you really want to know what I was thinking?" I asked, moving closer to him and my grandson.

"Oh, God! Do I really want to know, Ma?" He chuckled. "Yeah, sure, go for it. What are you thinking about?"

"I'm thinking that today is a perfect day—the weather, the water, being here with my family—I'm having one perfect day."

Yes, it was going to be okay.

My son and I have learned how to talk to one another. We have learned how to express our wants and needs with respect for the other's feelings and not in fear of them. It was not an easy path. It was difficult and painful and stressful for *both* of us. It took some real commitment and determination to hang in there with each other because we really hit some hard spots.

But today our relationship is better than ever. We know it will do nothing but grow because we genuinely love each other and are committed to making this relationship strong.

We came out of the getting-to-know-you process with a couple of those dings and scratches Steve told me about. We may have even experienced a dent or two. But I am sure my son would agree with me that it was worth putting up with the difficulties of building a relationship backward for the rewards of a future that includes both of us.

Steve and I bonded so many years ago as I talked to him inside my belly on the beaches of Atlantic City, as I hummed him to sleep at night in the darkness of that home for unwed mothers, as I cradled him in my arms in that hospital room and ran my fingers across his soft, downy hair and kissed his fingers and toes.

Mother and son.

He's a part of me—and I'm a part of him—the parts that were missing from both of us. Now we are both complete and whole with no more unanswered questions tormenting us through time.

Steve summed it up best that very first weekend when his brother, David, and I traveled to meet him. Although significantly more time has passed since he initially wrote these words, these excerpts from Steve's Facebook page, posted back on April 15, 2012, express the truth of our relationship both then and now better than I ever could.

My Mom and brother are back home safe and sound after what has turned out to be the best six days of my life!!! Truth be told, I honestly feel like my life is just beginning in so many ways. The excitement of knowing, after all these years, who

I am and where I came from, and looking forward to meeting all of the aunts, uncles, and cousins I now know that I have, will be an awesome experience.

I have to say that meeting my Mom after all these years has filled my heart with a love that I can hardly explain. I miss her so much already. So thankful also to meet David, my little brother, who was just awesome in so many ways, and I look forward to someday meeting my other brother, Dan, and his family. In my humble opinion, if there ever was a modern-day miracle, I truly believe this was it!!!

To all of my friends and family (especially my new members) who have had such kind words and were so happy and supported me, I just want to say Thank You, and stay tuned, this amazing story has just begun and I couldn't be happier!!

This adoption reunion has been a remarkable experience for not only my son and me, but also for our families and our friends.

Dan, Dave, and Steve have not only "friended" each other on Facebook, but are now an active part of each other's lives.

On a recent Labor Day weekend, I sat with Nancy and Joe on Steve's back porch. We found ourselves engaged in a rambling, fun conversation that covered everything from recipes for potato salad to current health issues to past vacations to making jewelry and other crafts. It was fun and comfortable and relaxed because we're family, the three of us. We are Steve Orlandi's parents and we have become friends.

Life has come full circle for me—from almost unbearable loss to precious treasure returned, from two sons and three grandchildren to three much-loved sons, three fabulous daughters-in-law, six grandchildren, three step-grandchildren, and a friendship with my son's parents.

As I approach the last stage of my life, I know one thing for certain. When my final moments on this earth come to pass, it won't be what house I lived in, what car I drove, what job I had, or how much money I put in the bank that will be on my mind. None of that matters in the end.

What matters is the lesson that God has taught all of us from the very beginning when He said, "Love one another as I have loved you."

Because that is all that really matters. The people. The relationships. The love.

Heaven isn't on Earth. I know that. But my heart is filled with such happiness and joy that I'm certain the good Lord has given me the tiniest glimpse of how wonderful heaven is really going to be. Until then, I will continue to cherish the memories we're building. I will hoard the moments.

In the evenings after dinner when I visit, I sit beside Steve in "Grandma's chair," which they bought for my birthday. We rock together, another thing both mother and son have in common. We enjoy the twinkling lights of the palm trees in each corner of the room. We listen to the cacophony of the frogs serenading us from the pond. We play country music and we talk the night away as we have done so many nights before.

Was it worth the journey? Am I happy I got that letter? Would I have called my son that night in April if I had it to do all over again?

I can't imagine doing anything else.

God is directing my life and leading me down the path He always intended for me. A path built by faith and filled with happiness and joy. I've learned to trust Him. I've learned to wait on Him because His time and His ways always work out for the best. It may have taken me forty years to get here. The journey may have been over rocky ground and riddled with pain. But I never journeyed alone.

God was always at my side even when I would choose to ignore Him, He was the first to have my back and He always will.

I'm in the bedroom and I can hear Steve running up the stairs. He stops at the top and looks at me through the open door.

"Hey, Ma, where ya been?" he asks. "We've got burgers on the grill and everybody's down by the pool."

"Okay, honey, I'll be right down."

He turns and disappears back down the stairs.

I finish what I was doing. As I turn to leave the room, I can hear Steve's voice in my mind and I smile.

Hey, Ma, where ya been?

Right here, son—for forty years—waiting for you.